A Spiral Way

A
Spiral
Way

How the Phonograph Changed Ethnography

Erika Brady

University Press of Mississippi / Jackson

www.upress.state.ms.us

Library of Congress Cataloging-in-Publication Data

Brady, Erika, 1952–
    A Spiral Way : how the phonograph changed ethnography / Erika
Brady.
        p.   cm.
    Includes bibliography references and index.
    ISBN 1-57806-173-3 (cloth : alk. paper). — ISBN 1-57806-174-1
(pbk. : alk. paper)
    1. Sound recordings in ethnology—History. 2. Sound recordings
in ethnomusicology—History. 3. Phonograph—History.
4. Phonocylinders—History. 5. Phonocylinders—Collectors and
collecting. I. Title.
GN348.B73 1999
305.8'0028'4—dc21   99-24533
                                                                    CIP

British Library Cataloging-in-Publication Data available

*The second strophe of "Quaerendo Invenietis," by Howard Nemerov, is used
by permission of Mrs. Howard Nemerov.*

For Frank B. Brady
wizard of my childhood
who shared with us his love
for the way things work.

It is a spiral way that trues my arc
Toward central silence and my unreached mark.
Singing and saying till his time be done,
The traveler does nothing. But the road goes on.

—HOWARD NEMEROV

Contents

Acknowledgments

I intended this book to be in part about gaps and silences—gaps in the picture we have created of participants in early ethnography, and the ironic silence surrounding the early use of the talking machine in that work. Through the Federal Cylinder Project, I took part in the later years of that story; it would have been neither possible nor appropriate to leave myself out of the account. Now that the account is written, I want to fill in a few more gaps and silences, acknowledging some of the many others involved in the tale.

Alan Jabbour and Robert Carneal hired me as a folklorist/recording technician at the Library of Congress in 1973. Each in his way took a chance on me, and each has since provided generous support and counsel. John Howell and Michael Donaldson were always on hand to bail me out of my technical scrapes. Their fellowship made the job a pleasure.

Joseph Hickerson and the late Gerald Parsons in the Archive of Folk Culture shared the documentary resources of the Library collections and added many insights into the personalities and occasional idiosyncrasies of the early collectors. Sam Brylawski, of the Recorded Sound Section, one of my oldest friends and co-workers at the Library, came through handsomely with assistance on this work. Gerald Gibson's research uncovered many technical and historical aspects of cylinder recording.

I owe a warm debt of gratitude to the employees of the American Folklife Center, and in particular to my fellow staff members on the Federal Cylinder Project for their expertise and their continued friendship, especially Thomas Vennum Jr., Ed Schupman, Judith Gray, and Dorothy Sara Lee.

A number of folklorists commented on various stages of the research and offered encouragement along the way, including Ruth M. Stone, Hasan El-Shamy, W. Edson Richmond, Mary Ellen Brown,

Rayna Green, Robert Georges, and Barbara Kirshenblatt-Gimblett. Their assistance was a powerful incentive. Above all, Rosemary Lévy Zumwalt's detailed, generous, and knowledgeable reading of the manuscript improved it in numberless ways, great and small.

I have been most fortunate in my colleagues, students, and friends at Western Kentucky University. David D. Lee, my dean, and Thomas P. Baldwin, my department head, and Michael Ann Williams, director of Programs in Folk Studies have been generous in allotting me the precious time necessary for writing. Fellow folklore faculty members Camilla Collins, Larry Danielson, Lynwood Montell, and Johnston A. K. Njoku have all helped the project along. Student assistants Erin Roth, Jacob Owen, Ann Ferrell, and Scott Sisco have gladly tracked down references, pounced on typos, and kept my files and my good cheer on track. Selina Langford, of Western's Library Public Services, was tireless in her pursuit of obscure sources through interlibrary loan.

Paula Fleming and David Burgevin of the Smithsonian Institution assisted with illustrations for the book under difficult circumstances.

Any project of this kind creates demands at home as well as at work. Here too I have been blessed. The pleasant custom of acknowledging the support of one's pets is now greeted with some sarcasm among the uncharitable; I can only regret that they have never made the acquaintance of Kittredge and Bubba, best of cats, who, like Pangur Ban in the old Irish poem, pursued their investigations with vigor and élan, while I followed my own more plodding track.

It was in the course of my work with the Federal Cylinder Project that I met my husband and friend, Nolan Porterfield. His unflagging encouragement and trenchant comments on the manuscript have been invaluable, but it has been above all the uncompromising quality and depth of his own scholarship, and the painstaking discipline underlying his graceful, seemingly effortless prose, which have set me a standard I despair of ever matching, but for which I am deeply grateful.

These days "home" extends well beyond the literal hearth, and my beloved mother has cheered me on by weekly phone calls, lately by means of e-mail, creating a virtual fireside that has warmed me to the heart. My debt to my father is only in part reflected in the book's dedication. The influence of his experience and his highly original take on technical matters has informed every stage of my involvement in early recordings. In addition, his reading of the manuscript was penetrating and thorough, with suggestions I have gladly accepted wherever possible.

When an involvement in a project extends over several decades, and the project content extends a century into the past, inevitably there will be those who have been part of the deal who remain unrecognized. To them, as well, I offer my thanks. One of the humbling revelations of this research has been how little we know of the uses to which our work may eventually be put. Ethnographers and performers left us much to ponder, but gaps and silences will always remain; the full story always remains to be told. I hope that the untold stories and the unrecognized participants whom I have inadvertently passed over will, through the agency of others, someday also take their place in the picture. The workers change, but the work, thank God, goes on.

A Spiral Way

Introduction   *"Fugitive Sound Waves," Fugitive Voices*

The imagination of Thomas Alva Edison was fertile but not fanciful. He was a forward-looking pragmatist. No sooner had he developed a working model for a talking machine than he was listing for entranced reporters the "illimitable possibilities" and "numerous probabilities" by which the so-called phonograph would improve the future of mankind, and, not in the least incidentally, reap a fortune for its inventor (Edison 1878:527). What a richly tinted vision of a new era he painted! Like many nineteenth-century optimists, he anticipated changes in the trappings and protocols of a familiar world, not the transformation of that world into something wholly new. His projections dwelt complacently on the twin realms of industry and domesticity so dear to the late-nineteenth-century spirit. For the improvement of one's hours of business, the phonograph would provide a tireless mechanical amanuensis: the businessman of the future would record his correspondence onto wax cylinders, from which a secretary would later type the letters. Outside the office, the phonograph would provide instruction in languages, serious entertainment through recordings of the best music, and perhaps—the genius of Edison stooped reluctantly to the thought—the voice of a child's doll (1878:531–36; Read and Welch 1959:11–24). The machine was a genie who would streamline the business world, and then enrich and enliven the hours of leisure purchased by this efficiency by capturing and preserving "fugitive sound waves" (Edison 1878:530).

A man of affairs and futurist whose mind only restlessly inhabited the present, Edison understandably overlooked in these vivid depictions a use for the phonograph that was intrinsically backward looking, one that would bring only slender profit to the infant recording industry. No gaudy campaign breathlessly promoted the phonograph as a tool to preserve the religious and aesthetic expressions of cultures undergoing radical change in the 1890s. Unheralded then, and largely overlooked now, this process of preservation nevertheless accomplished a considerable task: professionals and devoted amateurs sought out and recorded the speech and music of cultures and communities the old ways of which were succumbing to the very world whose advent trumpeted from the phonograph's great horn. In the physical sense intended by Edison, all sound is "fugitive," the cyclic disturbance of the air represented by the image of "waves" is by definition ephemeral, decaying immediately. But these voices ethnographically preserved in the wax of his cylinders were "fugitive" in a more profound historical sense. Their content and meaning were under assault from the new world the inventor and his followers were creating. The phonograph as a force in popular culture accelerated the process of corruption and decay of traditional ways of life—or so claimed many ethnographers. Ironically, many chose the phonograph—the very agent of corruption—as their tool of choice in preserving the disappearing remnants of those ways.

The use of the phonograph in the study of culture contributed little to the growth of the recording industry, but the availability of the phonograph as a tool expanded the range, focus, and methods of academic engagement with the scientific study of culture. From the time Jesse Walter Fewkes published his account of the usefulness of the phonograph on a collecting trip to Calais, Maine, in 1890, no ethnographer tackling fieldwork could take the notebook-and-pencil method of recording for granted as the only possible method of documenting verbal and musical forms of expression.[1] Although the phonograph and later means of technical sound recording were sometimes rejected for economic, practical, or philosophical reasons, such means still represented an option to be considered and evaluated in terms of the potential effect on the fieldwork encounter itself, and in terms of the value of the documentary evidence preserved in that medium. For many, the chance to use the phonograph was not automatic: many factors, including practicality, compatibility with a collector's self-image as a fieldworker, and complex theoretical and conceptual concerns, affected the decisions. Examination of the use of the machine can reveal much concerning motives as well as methods in the fields of folklore and anthropology during a critical era in their development.

Members of the ethnographic areas of study will recognize what other readers may surmise: the disciplines of folklore and anthropology share an uneasy historical connection the unraveling of which would dismay the most intrepid specialist in kinship relations. Although the study of folklore as such antedates the study of anthropology and is practiced in the United States as an independent academic discipline, histories of anthropology generally consider "folklore" as the subset of anthropological study devoted to formularized verbal and musical forms such as myth, song, and so forth as found in non-Western cultures. Indeed, many of the "fathers" and "mothers" of American anthropology such as Franz Boas, Alfred Kroeber, Robert Lowie, Ruth Benedict, and Elsie Clews Parsons designated their calling "ethnology," considering themselves "folklorists" in those instances when they were working with forms of expression that they considered "folklore." In contrast to these "anthropological folklorists," "literary folklorists" such as George Lyman Kittredge, Stith Thompson, John A. Lomax, and Archer Taylor derived their intellectual lineage from the tradition of Johann Gottfried von Herder, Jakob and Wilhelm Grimm, and Francis James Child, in which non-elite expressive forms such as ballad, folksong, folktale, riddle, and proverb in Western culture were examined primarily to reveal their formal patterns and historical interrelationships, rather than in terms of their role in the larger patterns of life within a community. The intricate and highly politicized rivalry between these two schools has been heroically disentangled by Rosemary Lévy Zumwalt, especially in relation to the study of the verbal and musical expressive forms the phonograph was well suited to preserve.

Scores of ethnographers and other collectors did accept the challenge of the new technology. Many were employed by the Bureau of American Ethnology or other federal agencies, whose collections were eventually deposited in the Library of Congress, housed in the office now known as the Archive of Folk Culture. Private collectors and those sponsored by universities and philanthropic organizations also contributed to the Library's holdings of early ethnographic recording on wax cylinder, making it now the largest single such collection in the country. It was while working for the Library of Congress that I first became concerned with the relationship between the phonograph and fieldwork. Hired with a bachelor's degree in folklore, I was trained by the Library sound engineers in preservation and duplication of early sound recordings, and I became a staff technician specializing in the

Figure I.1. Erika Brady recording cylinder to tape, 1979. Carl Fleischhauer, Library of Congress.

unique problems posed by the Library's immense collection of field-work recorded on wire, disc, and tape, as well as wax.

When I began my work at the Library, inquiries and orders I filled were almost always for members of the academic community—primarily folklorists, anthropologists, and ethnomusicologists. But in the course of the 1970s, an important new audience emerged, requiring us to expand our operations and rethink many of our assumptions concerning the use of the material. Alan Jabbour, director of the American Folklife Center at the Library of Congress, recalled the onset of this unexpected grassroots interest in the old recordings:

> Like a wildfire, the passion for searching out, embracing, and elaborating upon one's roots spread through the United States during the Bicentennial era. Nowhere has this renewed passion and concern been more visible than with American Indians, and the Folk Archive found itself the recipient of an increasing number of inquiries from Indian tribes, organizations, and individuals about those early cylinder recordings. To the scholars they provided fascinating documents for the study of cultural history; but for the spiritual heirs of the traditions the cylinders documented, the recordings had the greater intimacy of being "somebody's grandfather." (Jabbour 1984:7)

In response to this stimulus, with the support of the Smithsonian Institution the American Folklife Center inaugurated the Federal Cylinder Project in 1979, including me on the team as technical consultant and researcher. The project's aim was to organize, catalog, preserve, and disseminate the content of the cylinders, contributing to both the work of scholars and the process of cultural renewal then taking place.

As the preservation and dissemination connected with this project progressed, I became increasingly perplexed at the use being made of the recordings I produced. The project often placed me in direct communication with researchers and members of community and tribal organizations who had ordered copies of the cylinder recordings. I began to realize that most contemporary scholars listening to the phonograph had a limited understanding of the mechanical means and the usual circumstances under which the recordings had been made. For example, folksong scholar Alan Lomax—who had, as a teenager, himself used a cylinder phonograph from time to time— urged that each recording be entered in his complex cantometric system of description and comparative analysis by distinctive feature. The significant characteristics used in cantometrics included size of ensemble, vocal quality, and use of instruments. It was troubling to me, however, that accounts of early fieldwork procedure suggest that collectors took into consideration the capabilities of the phonograph and sometimes chose to limit ensemble size and use of instrumentation, selecting singers whose vocal quality would register best on the cylinders. They sought technical excellence as well as representation of the norms of performance within a culture. Without taking into account the nature of cylinder recordings, any tabulation of characteristics made from these collections would have been hopelessly skewed. The scope of the Federal Cylinder Project did not encompass such an accommodation, so the cantometric analysis of the cylinder material was not undertaken, to Lomax's lasting regret.

Another scholar visiting the Archive shared with me his conclusion that Frances Densmore was in the forefront of technical innovation in ethnographic fieldwork. "How so?" I asked. "Well, she writes that she made some of her earliest recordings on disc." This revelation astonished me as much as it would have Densmore herself, placing her a good forty years ahead of any available technology adaptable for fieldwork. A gentle probe disclosed that his evidence for her precocity was her frequent use of the noun "records" throughout her career to describe her collected material. He was not aware that at the time Densmore wrote of her "records," the term "record" described any kind of sound recording—cylinder, wire, or disc. (Compare, for example, those who persist in the mid-1990s in referring to compact discs as "albums"—a term that in its literal sense has now been obsolete for several technical generations.) Yet another user of the collection, a respected ethnomusicologist, was prepared to conclude on the basis of listening to archival recordings that American Indian songs at the turn of the century averaged four to six minutes in length—the duration of most cylinder recordings.

I was dismayed. Was I spending my workdays on tedious and demanding technical tasks only to see them result in misleading scholarship and mistaken assumptions? I began to consider ways in which the technical capabilities of the cylinder phonograph, once well understood but now forgotten, had affected the content. Initially my intention was no more ambitious than to provide a kind of "retrospective manual" for users of wax cylinders: a summary of the characteristics of the early phonograph and its use in fieldwork that would enhance the understanding of the capabilities and limitations of the machine as an ethnographic tool.

Once embarked on this investigation, however, I realized that even a preliminary analysis of the impact of the cylinder phonograph on folklore and anthropology would require more than a study of the machine's technical limitations. Robert A. Georges and Michael Owen Jones demonstrated in their important book, *People Studying People,* that all fieldwork research on aspects of culture inevitably takes place within a web of complex human determinants. Georges and Jones focused their inquiry on the effect of recognized and unrecognized motives and anxieties upon the fieldworker, as well as the complex negotiation of role and procedure that must take place with the native performer/consultant before the work goes forward. Would the introduction of a mechanical "third presence" in the form of a phonograph have any discernible consequences in the recording of fieldwork, or was its presence neutral, as inconsequential as the brand of pencil or the spacing of lines in a steno pad in transcription by hand?

I believe that the introduction of a "mechanical presence" embodied in the recording both determined the form in which information was preserved and significantly altered the balance of the entire fieldwork interaction. Its use affected both fieldworker and performer, sometimes supporting and sometimes subverting the collaborative aspect of their efforts. No matter how routine or apparently unconsidered the methods employed in fieldwork might appear, these methods have meaning in a search for full understanding of the process and, more important, for accurate evaluation of the process's results. The employment of the phonograph implied a set of choices made by the collector based on training, disposition, and intellectual assumptions; the cooperation of the performer implied choices based on personal and cultural criteria no less complex and serious. Although the cylinder phonograph was hailed as a scientific, objective tool, its use reflects a full measure of characteristics resulting from subjective motivations, conscious and unconscious, of collector and performer. Examination of the use of the phonograph in this light supplements the work of such recent historians of ethnography as George W. Stocking, Curtis M. Hinsley Jr., Joan Mark, Rosemary Lévy Zumwalt, Simon Bronner, and Desley Deacon.

The importance of an examination of the role of the phonograph in fieldwork is not merely historical, however. An investigation of early responses to the phonograph by ethnographers and their subjects illuminates many of the central questions still faced by fieldworkers concerning their role in the field and their self-presentation in reporting their findings, which only in the last twenty years have received open and systematic scholarly attention, in the challenging studies of a host of scholars such as Dennison Nash and Ronald Wintrob, Jay Ruby and Barbara Meyerhoff, James Clifford and George E. Marcus, Robert A. Georges and Michael Owen Jones, John Van Maanen, Elaine Lawless, John Dorst, Paul Stoller, and Michael A. Jackson. Acceptance or rejection of the device inevitably involved more than questions of expediency or personal taste. Issues concerning the importance of "text," the nature of performance context, and the researcher's perception of self in relation to the community being studied and in relation to the audience of his or her published works, all played a part in institutional and individual decisions concerning use of the phonograph. An examination of these decisions can tell us much not only concerning the history of anthropology and folklore as they were emerging as professional disciplines, but also concerning their current practice.

One of the most compelling emergent areas in folklore and anthropology in recent years has been a renewed attention to cultural implications implicit in sense perception. In addition to elucidating aspects of fieldwork, examination of the introduction of the phonograph to the American public and its subsequent use in recording native peoples in the field can provide an empirical testing ground for critical issues central to contemporary scholarly discourse even beyond the ethnographic disciplines. The brilliant "neo-evolutionist" studies initiated by Albert B. Lord, Walter Ong, and Marshall McLuhan that examine the phenomenology of the transitions from orality to literacy, literacy to print, and print to electronic communication draw on multiple sources for their broadly based conclusions (Lord 1960; Ong 1967,

1982; McLuhan 1962). Much as Elizabeth Eisenstein's comprehensive examination of the cultural and intellectual consequences of the invention of the printing press has offered a welcome degree of specificity to this discussion (1979), the documented circumstances surrounding the recent introduction of another revolutionary medium of communication, the phonograph—something quite new in the human "sensorium"—offer a valuable, highly specific proving ground in which to test the assumptions that underlie these works.

We will first examine the history and technical workings of the phonograph, with special attention to its remarkable effect upon its early audiences. The invention was publicized extensively and was a phenomena so utterly new that its effect on both fieldworkers and members of native cultures must be taken into account. We will then take up the state of ethnography in its various forms at the time of the phonograph's invention, and the impact—or lack of impact—the device had on fieldwork practice. A more detailed investigation of the reaction and attitudes of collectors and singers will follow, looking at the recorded performance as a complex cooperative process integrating the objectives of singer and collector. Examination of the changes in ethnography brought about by the phonograph can tell us much about the era of its invention—and our own.

1

The Talking Machine
A Marvelous Inevitability

> Just tried experiment with diaphragm having an embossed point
> and held against a paraffin paper moving rapidly. The spkg [speaking]
> vibrations are indented nicely and there is no doubt that I shall be able
> to store up and reproduce automatically at any future time the human
> voice perfectly.
>
> *Thomas Alva Edison, from notes dated July 18, 1877[1]*

Surprise, astonishment, awe, wonder: first reactions to the
phonograph's voice describe a shock almost visceral in its intensity.
Writing of his initial test of the invention, Thomas Alva Edison recalled
his own amazement: "I was never so taken aback in my life!" (Read
and Welch 1959:107–9). Yet though the machine was a marvel on
first encounter, its appearance at the end of the nineteenth century
was, in a broader historical sense, a marvelous inevitability—the cul-
mination of a host of technical and intellectual concerns that not only
represented a revolution in means of human communication, but also
brought about a radical reconceptualization of what human communication means.

The phonograph was distinctively the product of nineteenth-
century scientific and social preoccupations; at the same time the
machine represented an innovation in a progression many centuries
old: the human attempt to override the ephemeral nature of the sensory impression, to capture the impressions of the moment in a form
that would not merely evoke impressionistically but replicate accurately that moment at will. The two senses most urgently pursued
were those central to the communication of meaning for most human

11

beings: sight and hearing. The physical properties of light and sound had long been postulated, and eighteenth-century philosophers such as Immanuel Kant had addressed many aspects of the phenomenology of sight and hearing, but it was a peculiarly nineteenth-century hybrid of physicist, physiologist, and experimental psychologist exemplified by such brilliant researchers as Joseph Fourier, Gustav Fechner, Hermann L. F. von Helmholtz, and Ernst Mach who initiated systematic scientific investigation of the nature of these senses—their capabilities, limitations, and the physiological and cognitive structures by which they are experienced.

The perception of sound in human experience is inextricably linked to meaning through the essentially oral/aural medium of language. While nineteenth-century scientists explored the nature of hearing in the laboratory, philologists and folklorists investigated many facets of verbal communication with equal imagination and vigor, not only in their libraries and studies but also in the wider laboratory of what came to be known as "the field," the practice known as "fieldwork," collecting living expressive forms such as folktale, epic, ballad, and proverb as data in their researches. Followers of the eighteenth-century historian-philosopher Johann Gottfried von Herder might take the Romantic path that led from his doorstep under the guidance of Wilhelm Grimm, celebrating language and music as the aesthetic foundation for national character, or the more systematic philological path pursued by his brother Jakob Grimm in comparing languages to determine structurally their historic and prehistoric cultural relationships, but both paths converged in their agreement over the importance of language and, secondarily, music, as expressive forms key to the most profound understanding of the present and past—forms only recently and imperfectly preserved in the written and musical notation.

The source of nineteenth-century Romantic preoccupation with language and music as keys to cultural character can be found in Herder in passages such as the following from "Excerpts from a Correspondence on Ossian and the Songs of Ancient Peoples," in which Herder delineated a manifesto that was to revolutionize the attitudes of intellectuals toward these hitherto ignored groups:

Know then that the more savage, that is, the more alive and free-dom-loving a people is . . . the more savage, that is, alive, free, sensuous, lyrically alive, its songs must be, if it has songs. The more distant a people is from artful cultivated thinking, language, and letters, the less will its songs be written for paper—dead literary verse. These arrows of a savage Apollo pierce hearts and carry soul and thoughts with them. The longer a song is to last, the stronger and more sensuous the rousers of the soul must be, in order to defy the powers of time and changing circumstances of centuries—what do you say to that? . . .

In more than one province I am acquainted with folksongs, regional songs, peasant songs that certainly lack nothing when it comes to liveliness and rhythm, naivete and strength of language. But who is collecting them? . . . A small collection of such songs from the mouth of each nation, about the noblest conditions and deeds of their lives, in their own language but at the same time properly understood and explained, accompanied by music: how much it would enliven the chapter that the student of man reads most eagerly in every travelogue, "the nature and customs of the people! their science and letters, their games and dances, their music and mythology!" All these would give us better concepts of the nation than we get through the gossip of a traveler or an "Our Father" copied down in their language. As a natural history describes plants and animals, so peoples depict themselves here. ([1765] 1972:229–30)

The invention of the phonograph more than a century later was instantly recognized as an opportunity to preserve objectively and accurately these patterns of human expression.

These great strides in scientific and scholarly understanding of language and related phenomena excited the intellectual elite, but it was the more sensational technical developments touted in popular journalism of the period that caught the imagination of most people—thrilling and dramatic inventions that collapsed long-accepted limitations of space and time. Not only did transportation by rail and steamboat enable individuals to travel with unprecedented ease and speed, but, even more dramatically, images and voices could be separated from their source to embark on their own peregrinations. Introduced in 1839, the daguerreotype used a mechanical facsimile of the structure of the eye to preserve the instant visual impression of a moment in a form that would, to use a favored poetic conceit of the period, "defy the tooth of time." The patenting of the telegraph in 1834 and the telephone in 1836 enabled verbal communication over great distance, virtually instantaneously. Suddenly it seemed that sights and sound could be transformed into malleable, transferable, flexible units capable of being immediately conveyed elsewhere, or compacted into treasurable keepsakes that bore the very traces of the observed moment in its lineaments.

Simon Bronner has explored the late Victorian preoccupation with "things" as one factor among others in the development of the study of folklore during the late nineteenth century (1986:1–38). Arguably, a particular class of items—those that Charles Sanders Peirce categorized as "indices"—held pride of place in the minds and hearts of the period, serving as both artifact and sign in a very specific way. Peirce, the preeminent American philosopher of the era and progenitor of the contemporary study of semiotics, categorized as an "index" any sign "which refers to the Object it denotes by virtue of being really affected [or caused] by that Object" (Clarke 1990:78).

The late nineteenth century was particularly obsessed at both the intellectual and the popular level with the acquisition and display of *indexic* items—objects directly connected, literally pointing to and derived from, their referent. At the academic level, it was during this period that the great public museums were established, replacing the private collections of wealthy aristocrats with repositories that became shrines to the prevailing mythologization of a collective present and a collective history—not just reminders, but actual physical survivals emblematic of what a nation was, and had been. The tangible items on display provided a physical indexic link with the recognized great moments, great ideas, and great individuals of the public past—from the accessioning of huge quantities of aboriginal pottery by the Smithsonian, to the acquisition and enshrining of George Washington's false teeth by the Daughters of the American Revolution. The records created by the phonograph fit perfectly into the accumulative, item-centered indexic focus of educational expositions, museums, and academic institutions, great and small, as a record of collective history.

At the popular level, this impulse toward accumulation of indexic objects accorded a very special and privileged value to those items that not only symbolically alluded to but were actually derived from or in contact with the subject or individual being commemorated. It was above all the era of *objets de sentiment,* the flamboyant and unembarrassed sacramentalization of personal history—a pattern particularly evident in the observance of mourning customs sanctifying physical items belonging to the departed. Sir James George Frazer characterized one of the two primary characteristics of "primitive" thought as "the law of contagion," according to which items once a part of, or in contact with, an object of power retained some of that object's potency. He had ample opportunity to observe devout nineteenth-century practitioners of this system of belief and customary practice all around him, at every social level. Queen Victoria preserved every item in her beloved consort Albert's bedroom exactly as though he would return to it nightly—a practice given a macabre fictional twist by Miss Haversham in Dickens's *Great Expectations,* who for decades maintained all the preparations for a wedding breakfast that never took place. The custom is given a poignant American frontier flavor in Huckleberry Finn's account of Emmeline Grangerford's bedroom, where no one slept, "kept trim and nice and all the things fixed in it the way she liked to have them when she was alive" (Twain [1884–85] 1967:124). One of the first uses of the phonograph recommended by Edison's company was the creation of a phonographic family album, with the explicit expectation that it would be used as part of the rituals of mourning for family members, especially children, who had "passed on before." For example, in a promotional book published by the National Phonograph Company, the fictional narrator recounts the following pathetic episode:

> My wife called on our next door neighbor the other day to sympathize with her over the loss of their eight-year-old boy. They had bought a Phonograph, by the way, immediately on hearing ours. Well, the conversation naturally was about the dear little fellow who had just crossed over the Dark River. And she could not stop talking to my wife about his pretty eyes and curly hair and laughing voice. "It's one of the

greatest consolations that I have these," she said, going to her record cabinet and carefully taking from it three of the wax cylinders, she put one on the machine. The next moment it was as if Harry was in the room. . . . His mother sat there with tears in her eyes, but with a joyous look on her face. "My precious first born," was all she said. And one of the first things my wife did when she came home that afternoon was to take our poor little youngster and make half a dozen records of his chatter and baby-talk right away. I fancy him listening to those "talks" twenty years from now! But should he be taken from us in the meanwhile, I know I'd hold them as my most highly prized possession. (*Phonograph* 1900:137–38)

The phonograph satisfied both sides of a central contradiction of late nineteenth-century Euro-American society. If the period was characterized by an eager and confident propulsion into a future that bedazzled with scientific and technical promise, it was also a period that, Janus-like, honored the backward gaze—sometimes sentimentally for its own sake, and sometimes as a form of self-congratulation. The preservation of the past provided means to measure how far civilized Europeans had come. Audiences especially relished displays that juxtaposed supposedly primitive forms of expression with modern technical ingenuity. Visitors to the World's Columbian Exposition in Chicago in 1893 were entranced by the sight of Benjamin Ives Gilman using the brand-new cylinder phonograph to record "exotic" representatives of non-Western societies presumed to be a window on civilization's primitive past, and readers of the humor magazine *Puck* were amused by the image of a caged "Professor Monk the Scientist" demonstrating the phonograph to natives depicted as more ape than human.

The invention of the phonograph improved upon the capabilities of the telephone and telegraph, two of the choicest marvels of the time. Marvelous as they were, these two devices were less remarkable than the phonograph in two respects: the communication they provided was ephemeral, and the linkage between transmitter and receiver was physically mediated by a wire; wireless telegraphy was not invented until 1896. It was Edison's genius to see the possibility of

Figure 1.1. "Professor Monk" and audience. *Puck* 35, no. 897 (1894).

severing the connecting wires and storing oral communication in a form that could be replayed again and again, identical each time. Sound separated from source represented a kind of wizardry difficult for a secular society to assimilate in any but poetic terms. A reporter from *Harper's Weekly* published the following typical rhapsody:

> If it were not that the days of belief in witchcraft are long since past, witch-hunters such as those who figured so conspicuously in the early history of our country would now find a rich harvest of victims in the Tribune building . . . The phonograph records the utterance of the human voice, and like a faithless confidante repeats every secret confided to it whenever requested to do so. It will talk, sing, whistle, sneeze, or perform any other

acoustic feat. With charming impartiality it will express itself in the divine strains of a lyric goddess, or use the startling vernacular of a street Arab. (Read and Welch 1959:21)

Edison's experience as a telegraph operator, his investigations resulting in the invention of the telegraphic repeater, and his grasp of the mechanical components of the telephone all suggested to him the possibility of mechanically reproducing sound. In an article for the *North American Review* published in 1888, he revealed the manner in which the idea came to him:

> I was engaged upon a machine intended to repeat Morse characters, which were recorded on paper by indentations that transferred their message to another circuit automatically, when passed under a tracing point connected with a circuit closing apparatus. In this machine, I found that when the cylinder carrying the indented paper was turned with great swiftness, it gave off a humming sound from the indentations—a musical, rhythmic sound resembling that of human talk heard indistinctly. This led me to try fitting a diaphragm to the machine which would receive the vibrations of sound-waves made by my voice when I talked to it, and register these vibrations upon an impressible material placed on the cylinder. The material selected for immediate use was paraffined paper, and the results obtained were excellent. The indentations on the cylinder, when rapidly revolved, caused a repetition of the original vibrations to reach the ear through a recorder, just as if the machine itself were speaking. I saw at once that the problem of registering human speech so that it could be repeated by mechanical means as often as might be desired, was solved. (Edison 1878:642)

In August of 1877, he roughed out a sketch from which his machinist John Kreusi constructed a prototype. Cranked by hand, the device would record sound on, and play back from, a cylindrical surface covered with tinfoil.

Kreusi's prototype was put to test in a memorable scene. Having bet a box of cigars against his crew that the device would work, Edison cranked as he recited "Mary Had a Little Lamb" into the mouthpiece, then adjusted the machine to play back. The machine reproduced his words quite intelligibly, as he learned from the amazed response of the men; because his hearing was so poor, Edison himself was at first uncertain of the success of the test. But successful it was, to an extent that disconcerted its inventor. He remarked years later, "I was always afraid of things that worked the first time" (Read and Welch 1959:107–9). He was not too taken aback to protect his interest in the machine promptly, however, and submitted a patent application that was approved in February of 1878 (Read and Welch 1959:16).[2] Almost immediately six hundred machines along the lines of the original prototype were manufactured and sold, although they were only toys, with little entertainment or practical value (Read and Welch 1959:20). The new wonder soon caught the attention of the press and the imagination of the public through demonstration sessions put on throughout the country.

The device patented by Edison in the late seventies was little more than a popular novelty. It served to enhance Edison's reputation as an inventor and to publicize the idea of a talking machine, but like the computer in the fifties and sixties of this century, it was a phenomenon more often marveled over than actually seen, used, or understood. Further technical developments were necessary before the machine would live up to the serious uses envisioned for it and the wide market awaiting it.

During the 1880s Edison's attention was diverted to the refinement of the electric light bulb, while other individuals actively sought to refine the phonograph as first marketed by Edison. As a result, Edison's companies did not place a commercially viable phonograph suitable for dictation and home entertainment on the market until 1888, when they introduced the Edison New Phonograph. By this time, local and national companies had accumulated numerous patents relating to almost every mechanical aspect of the device. During the early years in which the phonograph was available to the public, it was the center of a litigious maelstrom that ultimately affected both the form taken by the machine as manufactured and the manner in which it was made available (Read and Welch 1959:25–57). Thus the demands of the public were not the only factors involved in the design and sale or lease of the phonograph in the late eighties and nineties.

From the simple tinfoil prototype to the carriage-trade models whose morning-glory horns grew luxuriantly from a mahogany base, all cylinder phonographs operated in the same fashion, using the same physical principles. The cylinder blank (succeeding tinfoil as the playing surface) was a hollow tube of a hardened wax substance about the consistency of soap or paraffin, the walls of which were between 3/16 and 1/4 of an inch thick. It was placed like a sleeve over an arm called a mandrel, which revolved at a steady speed. Suspended over the cylinder on the mandrel was a tonearm, which moved across the surface of the cylinder on a track determined by a drive screw. This drive screw was turned by the same power source revolving the mandrel. The tonearm, consisting of a horn mounted over a recording head, was the "scribe" that cut a spiral groove into the turning surface of the cylinder.

In performing for the phonograph, the subject directed the voice

Figure 1.2. Edison Standard Phonograph with horn. Library of Congress.

down the horn, the taper of which intensified and directed the energy of the sound waves, focusing them on a thin plate slightly larger than a quarter, made of a responsive substance such as glass, copper, or mica, serving as a diaphragm. The diaphragm vibrated to the pulse of the waves of sound, transmitting these vibrations to a small needle set between the bottom of the diaphragm and the surface of the revolving wax cylinder. As a result of these vibrations, the spiral groove cut on the surface of the wax was not a smooth trough but a series of irregular indentations. The pattern of this "hill and dale" groove varied according to the force and frequency of the sound waves.

When the tonearm was drawn back to the starting point of the indented groove and the cutting stylus replaced with a blunter playback needle, the tip retraced the irregularities of the groove created in recording and transmitted these to the diaphragm, the vibrations of which crudely recapitulated the movements of the original sound waves that had created the recording. These were transmitted through ear tubes or a horn to the listener, who easily recognized the aural image of the voice as it had been produced the moment before.

The type of machine placed on the market in 1888 was modest in size, no larger than the typewriters or sewing machines of the period. In its wooden carrying case, it weighed between thirty and thirty-five pounds: not a negligible weight, but easy enough to carry by its handle with one hand. The machine was operated by means of a spring- or battery-powered motor, a treadle identical to those used for sewing machines at the time, by hand, or by water power. The tinfoil cylinder surface of the original machine designed by Edison was replaced by a cylindrical wax sleeve commonly 4 inches in length and 2¼ inches in diameter, sturdy enough to withstand handling and soft enough to take the impression of the stylus. These cylinders were purchased blank; once they had been recorded, they could be shaved and reused.

The quality of such cylinders along with the sensitivity of the diaphragm determined the fidelity of the recordings; the length of the cylinders along with the pitch (grooves per inch) of the drive screw and speed of revolution determined how long a program could be recorded. In general, a 4-inch cylinder could optimally record between three and four minutes of program, and could record up to five minutes with some diminution of quality if the operator decreased the revolutions per minute by adjusting the machine.

By 1896 virtually all the refinements of design of the phonograph that would affect its usefulness as a tool in fieldwork had been introduced. In 1890, 6-inch cylinders were placed on the market—an important innovation increasing the amount of program time available on a single cylinder to as much as nine minutes. In general, the same machine could not play both 4-inch and 6-inch cylinders. Both sizes were used in fieldwork recordings through the mid-1930s. In 1894, American Gramophone introduced a spring-driven machine, and in 1896 the Edison companies followed suit. These crank-wound machines were exceptionally reliable, providing the user with a power source independent of heavy batteries or fluctuating house current. This was a particularly important innovation for the fieldworker, who could now easily transport a self-contained machine into virtually any environment to record.

Perhaps more important than design improvements, however, was the gradually diminishing cost. By 1896 a user could spend the same forty dollars that in 1890 had enabled him to lease the use of a hand-powered machine for a year to purchase a state-of-the-art Edison Spring Motor phonograph. As long as Thomas Edison insisted that the primary use of the phonograph was as a business tool, his companies clung to the marketing gambit of leasing machines on an annual basis, on the model of leasing telephones. But by 1896, the phonograph's primary market was clearly established: it was to be, above all, a source of entertainment in the home.

The phonograph sold best when it was advertised as an item no comfortable and up-to-date home could be without, as essential as the parlor piano. Edison gave up the preeminence of the business use of the phonograph with great reluctance; a pragmatist with poor hearing and limited taste in music, he insisted in a memorandum to his associate Alfred O. Tate in 1894, "Tate—I don't want the phonograph sold for amusement purposes, it is not a toy. I want it sold for business purposes only" (Read and Welch 1959:55). But as a businessman Edison could not ignore the locus of the profits. He soon saw that profits were in the sale rather than lease of machines and in distribution of prerecorded musical, educational, and novelty selections as well. By 1900, promotional material targeted men, women, and children as users, the location emphatically the home parlor. In one especially thorough introduction to the machine, purchasers were encouraged toward the original educational and business-oriented uses but also were instructed in more frivolous pursuits by the example of the fictitious Mr. Openeer and his wife:

> Last Christmas my wife and I were invited to a house party at Larchmont, New York. The gray afternoon was deepening into dim dusk as the sleigh left the little station, and the cold was intense. Our fifteen minutes' ride to the home of our host chilled us through and through, and as we fumbled with wraps and gloves in the silent hall of the house, our feelings were divided between personal discomfort and wonderment that no one was there to greet us. Suddenly there piped up a thin little voice seeming to come from nowhere. It grew louder and stronger and we heard "Merry Christmas, merry, merry Christmas. Welcome Mr. Openeer; we are glad to see you. Welcome, Mrs. Openeer; how is the baby? How did you leave Ponjo?" (Ponjo is our dog.) . . . Astonishment gave way to curiousity, and we drew aside a curtain and found the cheery speaker to be— a Phonograph.

The device provides a series of delightful pastimes, including a "Voice Guessing game," recording of guests' musical and rhetorical performances, and playing with "boughten records":

> Our host told us confidentially that had he engaged the artists, performers, and bands to appear in person, a thousand dollars would have been a reasonable price for the entertainment that was provided for less than a tenth of that sum . . . I have since bought a Phonograph for myself; and have been repaid a hundred times for the investment, by the fun and entertainment I've gotten out of it. (*Phonograph* 1900:135–37)

The Openeers' own "fun and entertainment" include painless language lessons, creation of a "friendship album" of recorded vocal contributions, Mr. Openeer's private unexpurgated collection of stories shared on the road among his fellow salesmen, and a genteel Phonograph Party at which guests were refreshed by molded ice-cream cylinders and gingersnaps shaped like phonograph horns (*Phonograph* 1900:135–51).

Despite the attraction of pastimes such as these, which depended on the recording capability of the home phonograph, the dominance of sales of prerecorded programs over blanks grew with every passing year, taking off in earnest once Edison and his competitors devised a means by which the program could be molded into the cylinders at the time of manufacture; until then, technically speaking the prerecorded cylinders were instantaneous in the sense that each one was first manufactured as a blank and then recorded or inscribed individually. Although initially all phonograph models available could both record and play back, the greater public demand for prerecorded programs produced a market for less expensive models designed specifically for excellent playback quality.

Disc records introduced in 1895 by Emile Berliner were from the start available almost exclusively with prerecorded programs—the disc machines available to the public could not record discs in the home. Not only did the disc format satisfy most buyers' basic requirements in a home entertainment machine, the discs themselves were more convenient to handle and store. Furthermore, the phonograph companies soon realized that a shift to prerecorded discs and disc phonographs represented a shrewd self-protective business move: industry magnates of the 1890s recognized that, since the disc format eliminated the possibility of home recording, the market for prerecorded discs would be assured, protected from uncontrolled duplication. By 1899 the disc was beginning to eclipse the cylinder in popularity (Read and Welch 1959:175). Once the Edison Diamond Disc phonograph was finally introduced in 1912, the disc was clearly the format of the future for the home entertainment recording industry (Proudfoot 1980:30).

Businessmen, educators, and, of course, fieldworkers in the areas of folklore and anthropology continued to constitute a small market for cylinder phonographs and cylinder blanks. Edison's companies remained doggedly faithful to these customers and to the few others who preferred cylinders for home entertainment, manufacturing machines and blanks alongside the more successful disc and disc phonographs long after such a policy paid off in anything but goodwill. Edison himself never really reconciled himself to the discs, which were plagued by inner groove audial distortion resulting from the torque of the tonearm—a problem with which audio engineers contend even when designing disc systems today. Edison had contemplated using discs and even tape in the earliest models of the phonograph but always believed that his first choice, the cylinder, was the best (Read and Welch 1959:175).

Pathé ceased production of cylinders and cylinder phonographs in 1910; Columbia in 1912. Edison reluctantly discontinued the home entertainment models of cylinder phonographs in 1913 but continued to produce blanks and prerecorded cylinders, promising loyalty to the estimated one million cylinder phonograph owners of the time (List 1958b:11–12). Both the Edison and Dictaphone companies continued manufacture of cylinder machines using a 6-inch blank for use in office dictation; these machines offered the fieldworker the advantages of the extended program time of the longer blanks but were dependent on an electrical power supply.

Because discs had taken over the home entertainment recording industry, used cylinder phonographs of the spring- driven pre-1913 variety were readily available. Technically obsolete but sturdy and easily repaired, they could be found in junk stores well into the 1930s. Some collectors preferred these older machines for fieldwork—George Herzog recommended their use as late as 1936, twenty-three years after their manufacture had ceased (1936:573–76). Other collectors were content with the electrically-driven Ediphone and Dictaphone type machines. By the late twenties and early thirties, however, ethnologists were beginning to examine the possibility of undertaking fieldwork using newly developed custom-built portable disc-recording equipment. The League of Nations publication reporting the recommendations of the first International Congress of Popular Arts, held in Prague in 1928, reveals that the plenary session resolved forcefully that it behooved each government to record its peoples' traditional songs and melodies, specifying that this recording should be on disc and not on wax (Institut Internationale de Coopération Intellectuelle 1934:7). In 1932, Robert Winslow Gordon borrowed an Amplion disc recorder to try in field trips in West Virginia, Kentucky, and Virginia, becoming one of the earliest American collectors to use the disc format in fieldwork (Kodish 1986:185–86).

The "portable" disc-recording machines could be transported only by automobile and were extremely expensive. John A. Lomax estimated that the combined weight of his first electrically-driven disc machine and its battery was about half a ton; in order to take the apparatus into the field in 1933 he had to tear out the backseat of his car and build a wooden framework for the different parts. But by 1937, a disc recorder owned by the Library of Congress weighed less than one hundred pounds and was purchased for a relatively modest $250 (Lomax 1937:58–59). By the close of the 1940s, when the war was over and fieldwork in anthropology and folklore was again possible, developments in wire and tape recording as well as disc showed immense new promise as new means of recording that would "defy the tooth of time." The era of the cylinder phonograph was over.

2

A Magic Speaking Object
Early Patterns of Response to the Phonograph

> Sound is a very special modality. We cannot handle it. We cannot push it away. We cannot turn our backs to it. We can close our eyes, hold our noses, withdraw from touch, refuse to taste. We cannot close our ears, though we can partly muffle them. Sound is the least controllable of all sense modalities, and it is this that is the medium of that most intricate of all evolutions, language.
>
> Julian Jaynes, *The Origin of Consciousness in the Breakdown of the Bicameral Mind*

Edison knew he had a blockbuster invention on his hands—a machine with literally unheard-of potential. Nothing, however, in his technical notes or subsequent promotional writings suggests that he reflected deeply on the radical challenge the device would make on the expectations and perceptions of those first exposed to it, including himself—"I was never so taken aback in my life!"—and his dumb-founded staff. His grasp of the physical properties of sound and the potential for its inscription in soft wax was thorough, but his understanding of the complex nature of hearing as human sense modality was—like his own hearing—indistinct, and his understanding of the potential effect of a technologically recorded sound medium on a human audience, limited.

Other great minds of Edison's era *had* taken up the deeper psychological and philosophical issues related to sense perception in general and hearing in particular. The German physicist and physiologist Hermann L. von Helmholtz (1821–1894), considered the founder of perceptual physiology, postulated "perception as hypothesis"—that is, perception understood as a process both learned and empirical, which occurs not as an organism's mere passive receptivity to stimuli but rather as an active construction of experience, a perceptual image (*Anschauungsbild*) created from existing internal knowledge and reminiscence (Helmholtz [1866] 1968:181). The workings of this so-called top-down processing of sense experience was further developed and refined by the brilliant Austrian physicist and experimental physiologist Ernst Mach ([1886] 1897).[1] According to these researchers, the "internal knowledge" that creates perception from sense experience includes social understandings of meaning and process, as well as understandings based on personal experience and observation—a conclusion providing the basis for relativistic examination of perception cross-culturally.[2] The invention of the phonograph, then, coincided with the experimental investigations that form the basis for all subsequent scientific research in the area of cultural differences in sense perception. Taking place at the same time as this seminal research, the responses to the new machine represent a fascinating "laboratory" for assumptions concerning cross-cultural and culture-specific aspects of hearing implicit in their findings, yielding some unexpected results.

First encounters with the phonograph did not occur in laboratory-pure settings, however, nor are the reports we have of these encounters necessarily objective accounts of the event, especially in cultural terms. Instead, we have anecdotal accounts: sensitive souls fainting with astonishment, savage tribal chiefs trembling in awe, countrified hicks fumbling for explanation. The major sources for such information are contemporary newspaper accounts, which were often reprinted later as filler for phonograph trade publications. Although these first-encounter narratives may initially have been more or less faithful to the outlines of a particular event in terms of content, their eventual reformulation of structure and style is in increasingly jocular terms. The reader, presumed to be in-the-know, was encouraged to view with complicit amusement and condescension those unfortunate, benighted souls still ignorant of Edison's amazing device. As the machine became increasingly familiar to the general American populace, these reports became increasingly humorous and anecdotal, portraying individuals' first responses as quaint, naive, or credulous, in the pattern of the formulaic "rube" story, such as the following account, originally appearing in the *Indianapolis Sun* in 1902:

> "Yes, sir," said Uncle Reuben, as the Phonograph stopped, "that's mighty good—mighty good!"
>
> "Just wait awhile," said the youth, as he slipped on another record, "and I'll explain it to you."
>
> "Oh, I understand it all right," responded Reuben, "Understand it all except one thing."
>
> "What's that?" asked the youth.
>
> "Well," answered Reuben with an abashed grin, "I understand how these sleight-of-hand fellers pull big rabbits out o' little hats, but I'll be danged if I understand how you git a full brass band in that box."[3]

Journalists dwelt on dramatic responses, copywriters emphasized aspects of the events that would sell phonographs, and ethnographers, by no means exempt from the ethnocentric bias reflected in journalistic and commercial accounts, glamorized their own role while romanticizing and marginalizing the attitude of their informants toward the machine. For example, anthropologist Jaime de Angelo remembered his Pit River acquaintance Sukmit's naive reluctance to perform, concerned that the white man's technology would be too much for his *damaagome,* a supernatural helper.

> He seemed dubious, torn two ways by his vanity and his fear of possible consequences. "See, suppose I put my song in the machine; now you go to Berkeley; sometime you play my song; my *damaagome,* he hear it, he say: Ha! my father is calling me, I better go and find him, maybe he needs me. . . . So he come here to Berkeley, strange place, maybe he get lost, maybe somebody steal him . . . then I get sick, maybe I die. . . ." "Aw! he couldn't hear that phonograph all the way from Alturas!" "Sure he can! Just like 'lectricity, it goes underground, but it don't need no wires." (1973:63)

Like many such accounts, de Angelo's parallels the "rube" story structurally, describing the subject's mingled attraction and anxiety, the operator's attempt at explanation, and the subject's concluding remark, a "punchline" that conveys the stubborn depth of the subject's misconception of the workings of the machine and implies the futility of bringing him to full understanding of it.

Proliferating in response to the commercial introduction of the phonograph and gradually fading away as the machine became a part of everyday life, these published anecdotes probably draw on a body of oral tradition as well as elaborated reporting of direct experience. They represent a variety of urban legend that typically clusters around mysterious new inventions—a narrative in which a new user grossly misunderstands the operation of the device. According to this pattern, as the invention becomes increasingly familiar, the misuser is ascribed an increasingly marginal social status in the accounts. A latter-day parallel is the urban legend of several years ago concerning the woman who attempts to dry her rain-soaked poodle by putting him in the microwave oven, where he explodes. As microwave ovens have become more and more common, the point of the legend seems to be focused less on the exotic and unfamiliar nature of the device and more on the ignorant nature of the misuser, who is more and more likely to be identified marginally or exotically as a foreign-born maid or a drug-impaired "hippie" baby-sitter.[4]

Careful examination of the available accounts of first impressions of the phonograph in the United States, the early uses to which the phonograph was put, and the attitudes and fancies that surrounded it in the American press indicate that the reaction to the phonograph among "technologically sophisticated" mainstream Americans was anything but blasé, and the initial impact of the machine upon them manifested itself in patterns precisely parallel to those remarked upon in the humorous fictional or factual accounts of first encounters with the phonograph in groups designated "outsider" or "primitive." The style of the humorous accounts, in fact, far more clearly reveals a projection of the fantasies and anxieties of the tellers' culture than an accurate picture of native and other nonmainstream cultures. Native and other informants brought their own cultural equipment to the experience of being recorded, enabling them to face the mechanical wonder with more nonchalance than the patronizing anecdotes give them credit for—sometimes with greater sangfroid and dignity than members of the culture intent on recording them. Robert H. Lowie recounts an illuminating observation made by Clark Wissler: "He had procured some phonograph records from the lips of an aged Blackfoot, and by way of making conversation, enlarged on the wonderful ability of the man who had invented this marvelous apparatus. The old man would have none of this; the inventor was not a whit abler than anyone else he contended, he merely had the good fortune of having the machine, with all its details, revealed to him by a supernatural being" (Lowie 1959:81).

Jesse Walter Fewkes admitted that he did not know what the men and women of Zuni thought of the phonograph on the occasion of his visit in 1890, but he was struck by the fact that most regarded the machine without fear. Some suggested that a small person must be inside; others believed that it was bewitched, but bewitched or not, it did not seem to excite much anxiety—to Fewkes's surprise (1890c:1094–98). Far from inflating the mystical or numinous properties of the phonograph, the Hopi visited by Fewkes in the late 1890s represented the machine in an irreverent send-up of Fewkes and his fieldwork procedure in the course of ritual clowning in celebration of the Basket Dance. A stovepipe representing the horn was placed on a table covered with a blanket, underneath which a clown was concealed. Another clown yelled into the pipe, and the hidden man responded with nonsense, while a third clown dressed as an "American" stood by and frantically scribbled on a piece of paper. The performance was a great hit (Fewkes 1899:87).[5] In contrast, it was participants in American mainstream culture who maintained an attitude of mythically charged wonder, albeit somewhat posed and affected, toward the phonograph and its inventor.

Regardless of one's cultural framework or technological experience, a first encounter with the phonograph was often a deeply unsettling occurrence. When the phonograph was demonstrated in 1878 before members of the National Academy of Sciences, hardly a naive group, several individuals in the audience fainted and one onlooker characterized the scene as diabolical (Conot 1979:109). Nausea and other manifestations of anxiety were not uncommon. Thomas Edison himself confessed that the successful first trial of the tinfoil phonograph left him breathless. Clearly, the phonograph was not merely another ingenious new invention to exclaim over; its reproduction of sound experientially challenged fundamental universal expectations concerning the nature of hearing in a profound and disturbing fashion.

Phenomenological examinations of hearing frequently allude to the "interiority" of auditory sensation. In a brilliant exploration of sound and language in the human sensorium, the Jesuit social historian Walter Ong suggests that "whereas sight situates the observer outside what he views, sound pours into the hearer. . . . When I hear, I gather sound simultaneously from every direction at once: I am at the center of my auditory world, which envelopes me, establishing me at a kind of core of sensation and existence" (1982:71–72). The musical theorist V. Zuckerkandl also emphasizes the uniquely intangible nature of hearing, noting that in the sensations of seeing, touching, and tasting, we are always directly aware of the object in which the sensation inheres; "tone is the only sensation not that of a thing" (1956:71).

These arguments are persuasive when applied to the special status accorded to hearing in human existence—its role in verbal communication and its consequent centrality in any extended experience of communality, and even its particular relationship to experience of the supernatural. But such arguments ignore a fundamental characteristic of hearing that is universally a part of human development. Although hearing may not be experienced as a sensory interaction with a "thing" in the same fashion as sight, touch, and taste, it *is* experienced most typically as a sensation having a specific source—a source understood to generate sound by means of visible movement, setting up the disturbance of the air, that which is heard. The coordination of hearing and sight begins virtually at birth, and the urge to achieve such coordination appears to be innate: even blind children will turn their eyes toward the source of a sound and fix their gaze there, although the eyes wander in the absence of sound stimulus

(Wertheimer 1961:1692). Jean Piaget and Bärbel Inhelder have demonstrated that at seven to nine months of age a normally developing child will associate sounds with visually appropriate movement and will actively continue to seek the source of the sound if the source-movement is masked (1969:10).

The phonograph produces recognizable sound patterns without the movements and appearance a listener has been conditioned since infancy to expect from the producer of such sounds, and without any connection or conduit to such a source. The telephone and pre-1896 telegraph, marvels in their day, at least provided new users with a slender physical connection with the distant source of sound communication—sufficient to rationalize their operation on the analogy of speaking tubes. One could envision the sound made small, traveling through the wires. No such reassurance linked the phonograph with the familiar. An initial reaction of confusion and disbelief appears to have been common to members of any cultural group. This confusion was the result of the violation of fundamental understandings concerning hearing developed in human beings from birth.

In Edison's era, resolution of the cognitive confusion provoked by a first encounter with the phonograph may have been more complex and unnerving for participants in a materialistic and technically knowledgeable culture such as that of the United States in Edison's era. Sociologist Edward C. Stewart, among others, has noted that, for the typical mainstream American then as now, operations do not simply "occur"; they require a source, agent, or cause. Even when the agent is identified, search may continue for the background of the action (1972:31)—a compulsion not necessarily shared by other groups, and one not easily satisfied by observation of a working phonograph.

For a first-time listener, the phonograph demanded a new and unfamiliar way of hearing in which the source of the sound was completely divorced from the usual accompanying sensory information derived from visual interpretation of movement. With its oversized horn and the peculiar intricacies of the tonearm and mandrel, which masked the tiny movements producing the sound, the machine did not resemble anything familiar on earth. Prior to the phonograph, virtually every attempt at a mechanical "speaking automaton" conceived or invented was given a human form, as though to reembody the sound, even when that form was not dictated by technical requirements (Carterette and Friedman 1978:28–29). In effect, the virgin encounter with the phonograph thrust an individual into a real-life folktale adventure: a meeting with a magic speaking object.[6]

How could contact between a tiny needle and a smoothly rotating cylinder re-create the varying melodies and rhythms of speech and music? The effect and the apparent cause seemed so utterly disproportionate that many attempted to rationalize its operation in nontechnical terms. The simplest and most common hypothesis, more figurative than literal, seems to have been the presence of a small person or ensemble inside or near the base of the machine. So common was this image that the Edison companies tried to capitalize on it commercially, promoting an advertising campaign intended to rival Victor's phenomenally successful representation of "His Master's Voice"—a campaign based on a sketch of a small boy crouched threateningly over a phonograph, an upraised axe in hand. A paean celebrates the first publication of this image in a solemn effusion of free verse:

> The National Phonograph Co. has immortalized
> "The Boy with the Axe"
> He is the substance of an idea
> The realism of the phonograph is expressed in
> his person, in his uplifted arm, in the
> poised Hatchet.
> He is "Looking for the Band."
> (Ph 4, no. 6 [1902]: 88, 90)

Happily, the child vandal never caught the imagination of the public as did the attentive terrier, and "The Boy with the Axe" was rapidly abandoned as a corporate symbol.

Rationalization took other forms as well. Alerted by the relative familiarity of the telephone and telegraph, suspicious first-time listeners searched for wires or tubes conveying sound from the cellar or adjoining room. Jaime de Angelo's informant Sukmit made

Figure 2.1. "Looking for the Band," National Phonograph Company advertisement, c. 1902. Reprinted courtesy of the Eastern National Park and Monument Association.

the informed and reasonable, though incorrect, surmise that something like electricity accounted for the recordings. Other listeners guessed that the effect was created by skillful ventriloquism or some other ruse. Folksinger Jean Ritchie's father purchased a talking machine from Sears, Roebuck in 1905, and took it around the environs of their Viper, Kentucky, home, playing commercial cylinders such as Whistling Rufus performing "Little Liza Jane" for a nickel a tune. Word would go around that "thars a man . . . has got a machine can talk and no person inside, it has a great round horn of silver in front."

> They were awful skeptical when I would set it up.
>
> "Some trickery som'ers," they'd say to one another.
>
> "Now you *know* ain't no little box like that can talk. That man's a pyore fool."
>
> And they'd watch my mouth to see that is wasn't me a-throwing my voice. (Ritchie 1963:73–75)

Once the initial shock of hearing sounds reproduced by a machine passed, initiates were often amazed at the accuracy with which vocal and instrumental variation was recorded. It was as though listeners felt that the machine ought to produce only a schematized or mechanical "music box" rendition of human performance. The early trade literature abounds in anecdotes gleaned from newspapers and elsewhere in which the sound of the phonograph is mistaken for live performance:

> Miss Lois Van Fleet, of this city [Bartow, Florida], recently visited her grandparents at Auburndale . . . taking with her a Standard and a lot of Gold Moulded Records that she had just purchased. Arriving in the night, she found that the household had retired. Smuggling her phonograph into the room occupied by her sister she started it off with "The Man Behind," "Uncle Sammy's March," and other fine selections. The old lady was awakened and concluded that it was a serenade by the village talent. She was surprised by the uncanny hour of their visit and the wonderful musical progress they had made. It occurred to her husband, Col. Foot, that something should be done in response to so fine an entertainment, saying "By Jove, Martha, I'm going to invite the boys in." "What!" says she, "in here! Us abed! Why Richard there's not a bit of cake in the house." Later she said, "I'm so sorry, for they sang and played beautifully and were the best behaved lot of boys it was ever my pleasure to meet."
>
> Moral:—Though the Phonograph "takes the cake," it does not eat it. (*NPh* 1, no. 3 [September 1904]: 7)

Another facetious narrative reported in a newspaper and picked up by the vigilant trade press takes place in a ladies' hotel, in which men's voices cause a flutter until the source is discovered to be a phonograph (*EPM* 4, no. 12 [1907]: 17). The Memorex company did not invent the concept underlying the contemporary slogan "Is it real or is it Memorex?"; numerous promotions dating at least back to the late nineties used the idea of a curtained stage behind which an audience supposes a live ensemble or soloist to be playing, only to have it dramatically revealed at last to have been a phonographic performance (*NPh* 2, no. 2 [June 1906]: 12). The "Memorex effect" was remarked in animals as well: many anecdotes were published in which the ready responsiveness of dogs, cats, horses, and even hens provided the humor. According to a 1906 account published in the *Saginaw Courier,* a farmer found his hens responded to the power of suggestion and increased their laying when he played back for them the sound of their own cackling; the only drawback to the productivity scheme was the necessary presence of someone in the coop at all times to change the cylinders (*EPM* 4, no. 4 [1906]: 11; see also *NPh* 2, no. 3 [September 1905]: 10; *NPh* 2, no. 8 [February 1906]: 10; *NPh* 3, no. 2 [August 1906]: 11; *NPh* 3, no. 3 [September 1906]: 10; *NPh* 3, no. 4 [October 1906]: 10; *EPM* 2, no. 5 [1904]: 12).

The fidelity of both dog and machine to the master's voice was caught above all in the image of the terrier Nipper, ear cocked to the Victrola, in one of the most successful corporate trademarks of all time: Francis Barraud's painting represents a graphic version of the then-familiar dog-and-phonograph anecdotes (Petts 1983).

This preoccupation of the auditory fidelity of the phonograph strikes modern readers of these accounts as far-fetched. To our ears, cylinder recordings sound tinny and flat, with a throbbing overlay of high-frequency hiss that could never be mistaken for ambient noise. And indeed, more critical accounts exist suggesting that the anecdotes concerning accuracy of the machine represent, if not commercially interested fabrications, at least the kind of enthusiastic hyperbole that greets any spectacularly new innovation. Ethnologist Alice Cunningham Fletcher tellingly compared the resistance she experienced in coming to appreciate Omaha music with her initial difficulty in "reaching beyond the noise" of phonographic recordings, including, as well, an illuminating comment on culture-specific patterns of perception of music more generally:

> I think I may safely say that I heard little or nothing of Indian music the first three or four times that I attended dances and festivals beyond a screaming downward movement that was gashed and torn by the vehemently beaten drum. The sound was distressing, and my interest in this music was not aroused until I perceived that this distress was peculiarly my own, everyone else was so enjoying himself (I was the only one of my race present) that I felt sure that something was eluding my ears; it was not rational that human beings should scream for hours, looking and acting as did these Indians before me, and the sounds they made not mean something more than mere noise. I therefore began to listen below the noise, much as one must listen to the phonograph, ignoring the sound of the machinery before the registered tones of the voice are caught. I have since watched Indians laboring with a like difficulty when their songs were rendered to them on the piano; their ears were accustomed to the *portamento* of the voices in the song, which was broken up by the hammers of the instrument on the strings, producing such confusion of sound that it was hard for the Indians to hear and recognize the tune. (Fletcher 1893:237)

However it was evaluated by a listener, the effect of the phonograph's accuracy was intensified when the recording was of the subject's *own* voice or performance being replayed. The wax cylinder phonograph was capable of making records as well as replaying pre-programmed records. Listeners, therefore, were offered an entirely new opportunity to hear themselves as others heard them. It was not always a gratifying experience. Audiences at early promotional demonstrations were challenged to try to outwit the phonograph by singing or playing a piece too difficult for the machine to follow. When these performances were reproduced relentlessly note for note, the performers were sometimes dismayed, as anecdotes of the following pattern indicate:

> An amateur flutist once stopped at a fair where a talking machine company had an elaborate exhibit, and showed such an interest in the

talking machine that the attendant thought a sale was imminent, and worked very hard to effect it.

"I see you have your flute with you," he said, finally. "Suppose you play a brief selection, and I will make a record of it, and you will then be able to hear the machine reproduce it exactly."

The suggestion pleased the amateur musician, and the idea was carried out.

"Is that an exact reproduction of my music?" he asked, when the tune was finished.

"It is," replied the attendant. "Do you wish to buy the talking machine?"

"No," said the other sadly, as he slowly moved away. "But I will sell the flute." (*EPM* 3, no. 3 [1905]: 13)

The brilliant conductor and pianist Hans von Bülow, who had every reason to be gratified by his own musicianship, upon hearing a cylinder recording of his own performance for the first time, fainted dead away (Gelatt 1977:39).

Anthropologist Edmund Carpenter has remarked that the self-reflecting capacity of new technological media often results in a mixture of fright and exhilaration in which people cover their mouths and duck their heads. He surmises that this reflex, which he regards as almost universal, is a response to a perceived symbolic abrogation of identity; the mouth is covered in a delayed attempt to avert the loss (1972:124). Despite the accuracy of the phonograph, however, listeners did not always immediately recognize themselves in the voice played back: Frances Densmore tells of one Native American woman who reacted to the replay of her performance with more chagrin than anxiety, demanding to know how a device could so swiftly have mastered a song that had taken her seven years to learn (Hofmann 1968:104).

Fieldworkers frequently reported a kind of synecdochic response to the phonograph in which it was characterized as a monstrous, unnatural Ear or Mouth. The curious gaping orifice of the phonograph horn, which both "listened" and "spoke," undoubtedly suggested this image, if not to the subjects themselves, then certainly to the ethnographers recounting the episodes. The figurative devouring of identity in the gaping maw of the machine seems to have been a recurrent disturbing image in accounts of first encounters. Collector Helen Heffron Roberts recalled a valued Karok singer who "was scared to death. I think he thought it was going to jump up and bite him" (Roberts 1979). John Avery Lomax remembered that, in the course of his Harvard Traveling Fellowship from 1908 through 1910, the horn of the phonograph into which singers directed the voice was regarded with particular suspicion: "I lost many singers because the cowboys didn't like the looks of it" (Lomax 1937:57). Jean Ritchie's father, Balis, complained that patrons of his phonographic demonstrations kept trying to "feed" the machine by tossing nickels down the horn (1963:75). An Australian phonograph amateur wrote to the *Edison Phonograph Monthly* in 1905 reporting that the aborigine Corroborree he attempted to record was only intermittently audible because the performers were uneasy with the machine and kept jumping back from the horn (*EPM* 2, no. 12 [1895]: 13).

Even after the first-time listener grasped the mechanical nature of the machine, some found the temptation to "reincarnate" the voice in the machine in terms of a metaphorical personality almost irresistible. Curiously, this pattern is much more marked among Euro-American users, and can seldom be inferred from reports concerning responses of native peoples. Although the rationalizing image of the little man in the machine was soon abandoned, the tendency to personify the machine remained. To some extent this represents a form of humor, a playing with the pretense of the machine-as-person, as in the 1878 sheet music "Song of Mr. Phonograph" credited to Professor H. A. H. von O'Graff:

> My name is Mr. Phonograph, and I'm not so very old
> My father's name is Edison, and I'm worth my weight in gold.
> The folks must yell into my mouth and now I'm saying what's true:
> For just speak to me and I'll speak it back, and you'll see I can talk like you.
> (Read and Welch 1959:479–81)

Figure 2.2. Cover to sheet music, "The Song of Mr. Phonograph," 1878. Library of Congress.

In routine use, the phonograph seems often to have been casually personified by its users. A demonstration cylinder recording made by Fewkes in late 1890 or early 1891 for a Passamaquoddy visitor from Calais, Maine, addresses "Mr. Phonograph" as a pleasantry to entertain his guest:

> Now Mr. Phonograph, let's try it again. The other cylinder which I had talked back at me, and frightened me a good deal, so that I didn't [use] that one.
>
> Tonight a Passa . . . a gentleman from the Passamaquoddy tribe is come over to see you and to hear the songs which were sung by Peter Selmore and Noel Joseph, and some of the stories which they told. I am very glad to say that you recorded the stories, which I obtained in Calais about a year ago, so nicely that he is able to understand them and I think that shows that the phonograph can keep these stories for a very long time.
>
> Now the phonograph is a talking machine. It was invented by Thomas Alva Edison, a native of New York. You can talk into it as fast as you like [spoken rapidly], or, you can speak . . . as . . . deliberately . . . as you . . . choose. In either case, it reproduces exactly what you say.
>
> Now, Mr. Phonograph, let us hear what I have recorded on the phonograph in order that we can see what you can do in English. I know you will do pretty well. Goodbye, Mr. Phonograph. [Whistles a few bars.] (Fewkes 1890–1891]

The urge to personify the machine as a compliant servant when it was working properly was matched by the urge to demonize it when it balked. The impulsive ethnologist Truman Michelson seemed to invite the revolt of material objects against him; one former student at George Washington University recalled him as a rotund, bouncy individual who invariably got one foot caught in a wire wastebasket while lecturing. When his machine failed in the course of his Piegan fieldwork, he exploded in ineffectual fury still vivid nearly a century later, threatening it with dreadful fates if it continued to balk. His interview subject breaks in on the tirade, serenely reminding Michelson "It does no good to get angry" (Judd 1967:47; Michelson 1911–1917).

This process of personification, playful or vituperative, does not suggest that mainstream American users invested the machine with personality in any serious sense. What it does suggest is their preoccupation with the machine as a kind of abiding presence in any interaction involving its use. Unlike later forms of recording, the phonograph demanded the full attention of a performer: one had to sing or speak directly into the horn in order to record effectively. The result must have been very much like the introduction of a third stubborn, sometimes uncooperative, and slightly deaf, presence into what otherwise would have been a normal conversational or performance dyad. The machine insistently and quite literally called attention to itself in ways that could be both diverting and frustrating for the operator. The practice of directly addressing the machine as do Fewkes and Michelson in the above examples was quite common[7] and represents a striking departure from the conventions of discourse in more familiar media: Victorian journalists and novelists conventionally apostrophized their readers but seldom the paper they wrote on.

But the perception of the phonograph-as-person—indeed, a "person" more honest and reliable than most—underlies court cases recorded in Boston, Brussels, and London in the early years of the century, in which phonograph recordings were introduced as unimpeachable witnesses for the prosecution, in the first two cases offering evidence of noise damage, and in the third demonstrating breach of contract. Although such mechanical testimony would have been as easy to falsify as that of a witness, the use of the apparent objectivity of an "object as witness" was highly credible. The machine could "speak" for the plaintiff or defendant like a person, but with the integrity of an unswayable thing (*EPM* 3, no. 11 [1906]: 12; *EPM* 5, no. 5 [1907]: 16; *EPM* 2, no. 12 [1905]: 13; *Ph* 4, no. 6 [April 1902]: 89; *NPh* 1, no. 3 [September 1904]: 6). One of the most popular mystery novels of all time, Agatha Christie's *The Murder of Roger Ackroyd*, turns on the use of a voice recorded on cylinder recording to obscure the time of the victim's death (1926). For American and European listeners, the phonograph evidently bore a kind of symbolic authority inhering in both its "human" and "inhuman" characteristics, and perhaps deriving as well from the intrinsic nature of sound and the meanings specifically assigned to hearing in Western cultures.

Much recent discussion of the phenomenology of hearing has focused on the ineluctable nature of the sense; it is the least controllable of all sense modalities, that which we can least avoid or turn from by will, even when the stimulus is as slight as the drip of a faucet or the whine of a fluorescent light. Indeed, the very concept of "will" appears to be tied with the sense of hearing in profound and complex ways: in most European languages, the word corresponding to "obedience" in English derives from the Latin phrase *ob audire,* literally, "to hear while facing [someone]." In Western European tradition, both conscience and temptation are conceptualized as voiced entities paradoxically separate from, but part of, the individual; a recent Gallup poll indicates that one out of ten Americans believe that they have been "talked to by the Devil" (Gallup and Newport 1991:141), suggesting that the "voice of temptation" may represent more than a figurative, symbolic construct to many. According to the self-styled "preposterous hypothesis" of psychologist Julian Jaynes, at one time human nature was bifurcated, with an "executive" portion that came to be characterized as external and divine, and a "follower" portion perceived internally as "self," the commands of the former being communicated to the latter as spoken, heard instruction. Without accepting the unpersuasive neurological claims of Jaynes's hypothesis, one can still readily concur with his proposition that the perception of one's self as an autonomous being, subject nonetheless to commands and suggestions from others, is an understanding both derived from and supported by the experience of hearing. Regardless of whether a culture privileges visual, auditory, or tangible sensation, the value accorded the *heard* experience occurs in relation to the value accorded the essential communal and communicative forms, speech and music.

In a very literal sense, sound *is* power—energy translated into molecular movement that resonates in the very person of the listener. As Walter Ong suggests, sound therefore uniquely invokes the mysterious, the transpersonal, the numinous as can no other stimulus

(1967:162–63). Anthropologists working in specific cultural communities have also suggested sound as a uniquely dynamic medium for the expression and experience of emotion; in Paul Stoller's words, "an open door to the comprehension of cultural sensation" (1989:104; see also Feld 1982:3). For reasons perhaps rooted in the organization of the human neurological system, percussive rhythm is associated cross-culturally with ritual states of transition ranging from formal shifts in life status (bells at wedding and funerals) to the intentionally evoked alterations of consciousness experienced in ecstatic religious trance (Needham [1967] 1979:311–37).

Even more potent is the perception of a disembodied human voice as mysterious, compelling, and possibly dangerous. Characterized in mainstream American society as "auditory hallucination," the experience of hearing discarnate voices occurs cross-culturally with a frequency that, like the effect of percussive rhythm, suggests an origin in the central nervous system; they are experienced even among the profoundly deaf (Rainer, Abdullah, and Altshuler 1970:449–65). Cultural attitudes toward these experiences vary widely, from the reverential awe accorded to divine messages, to the imputation of mental illness. Auditory hallucinations are in fact typical of schizophrenia, occurring with statistically greater frequency than visual hallucinations. Nonetheless, they apparently also occur among normal individuals in the United States, Western Europe, and elsewhere, although the stigma attached to such experiences hampers any reliable systematic inquiry (Bleuler 1950:97–99).

This stigma attached to auditory hallucination could have been one factor in the somewhat exaggerated response to the phonograph observable among mainstream Americans on first encountering the machine. A straightforward and uncomplicated first response to the phonograph may have been easier in cultures in which the supernatural offered a viable explanation for mysterious disembodied voices. This is not to suggest, of course, that the voice of the phonograph immediately and directly suggested a supernatural explanation; indeed, it is the *lack* of such a culturally available explanation, coupled with the puzzling and indecipherable operation of the machine, that evoked astonishment and awe at the invention, an almost obsessive poetic insistence on personification of the machine, and the bestowing of the symbolic status of "wizard" on its inventor.

Whether beneficent or demonic, the personification of "Mr. Phonograph" by mainstream American users was powerful, recalling the folktale motifs describing a "magic speaking object," "speaking image," or "magic automata" (Thompson D1610; D1610.21; D1620). Edison's public relations staff was more than willing to cast the machine in their own heavy-handed Arabian Nights scenario. The following torrent of archaicized rhetoric and others like it were pre-recorded onto cylinders distributed to sales locations, to be replayed for potential customers:

BEHOLD THE SLAVE OF THE RING!

I am the Genii of Entertainment, created by the Great Wizard of the New World to delight him who possesses the ring.

Wouldst thou have melody?

Place thy ring upon my finger and I will sing for thee a tender song of love.

Or wouldst thou prefer merry tales and joyous laughter? These I can give thee until thy heart shall swell with happiness.

Perchance thou wouldst yield thy members to the rhythmic dance?

Then I can sound the harmonies that will float thy form through space e'en as the thistleblow rides the bosom of the breeze. (*EPM* 3, no. 7 [1905]: 3)

The quasi-supernatural authority of the voice of the phonograph was not the only characteristic of the new medium that absorbed and disconcerted listeners. In European and American cultures, hearing has been poetically and philosophically understood as the most ephemeral and evocative of sensory impressions, retrievable only through the mutable workings of memory. Western writers and thinkers in an unbroken line extending to St. Augustine back through Aristotle portray memory as a voiced entity. Marcel Proust writes figuratively of voices trapped in an inanimate object, lost to us unless we unwork the magic. "Then they start and tremble, they call us by their name, and as soon as we have recognized their voice, the spell is broken." The poignancy of this image lies in Proust's suggestion that this moment is a fairy-tale instant that for most of us never arrives—a finality that demonstrates the emphasis on closure that Walter Ong attributes to literate cultures, the past regarded as fixed, unchanging, and effectively irretrievable except through the flat, reduced, and unsatisfactory medium of print (1982:132–35). But the wax cylinder, crude as it was, challenged the finality of this image, offering just such a spell to release the lost voices. An inanimate object, the cylinder bore the traces of past events in its very grooves and was capable of reanimating the events' lost voices and wrenching time out of the linear conformation familiar to the Western mind, projecting past into present. What had been a dreamer's conceit was made uncannily real in the phonograph.

Edward T. Hall and Barre Toelken, among others, have observed that the American perception of time, like that of Europeans, tends to be linear: whereas other cultures may perceive time as a cyclic or episodic continuity, Europeans and Americans tend to perceive events as occurring in a given order within a continuum extending from creation to the apocalypse (Hall 1959:140–48; Toelken 1976:16–17). The stir caused by the phonograph among mainstream Americans may have stemmed in part from its apparent challenge to the perception of the inexorably unrepeatable nature of events in time.

This power to preserve the past was immediately translated into concrete and personal terms by Edison's writers when the machine became available commercially—especially once the strength of the "parlor market" outside the business world was established. One of the earliest home uses recommended for the phonograph was the creation of a family album of voices compiled explicitly to provide comfort should a member of the family die (*Ph* 1900:137–38). The very iconography of the phonograph was colored by what now seems to us a morbid concern with voices of the dead: a persistent contemporary legend dating from the unveiling of the painting "His Master's Voice" claims incorrectly that the original work included the dim outlines of a coffin in the background behind the attentive terrier and the machine, creating a visual variant of the many accounts of dogs faithful to dead masters.[8] Trade journals of the period report

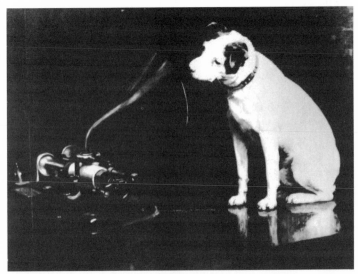

Figure 2.3. "His Master's Voice": An early image depicting Nipper with the cylinder phonograph. Library of Congress.

many accounts of men and women participating in their own funerals by means of the cylinder phonograph by singing their own anthem or delivering their own eulogy (*EPM* 3, no. 2 [1905]: 10; *EPM* 3, no. 3 [1905]: 12; *NPh* 2, no. 11 [May 1906]: 7; *EPM* 4, no. 2 [1906]: 10).

A publication of the National Phonograph Company in 1900 introducing new owners to the possibilities of the phonograph included a fictional set of papers penned by "Mr. Openeer." The usually breezy tone of the piece modulates briefly to a solemn key in a section in which the recovery on cylinder of a voice lost to death is placed in the context of the recent Spanish-American War:

> The hot and bloody work before Santiago, in Cuba, has made one of my wife's Voice Album records of inestimable value. Young Smith, of the 71st, New York, was my cousin, and one of the first to try the effect of his voice on a wax cylinder. His name comes out loud and clear, and then these words:
>
> "Of all the fish in sea or lake
> The bloomin' codfish takes the cake."

It's funny, but it's sad, too; for poor Smith was shot through the lungs with a Mauser bullet and died seven days afterward. When his father learned of the record, he bought the finest, most expensive Phonograph to be had, and we gave him our cylinder, taking several copies or duplicates of it for ourselves and his friends . . . the copies we made were plain enough for us to distinguish poor Bert's voice, and we are proud of it, I can tell you, not only for the satisfaction of having a *hero* record in our collection, but also that we were able to be of service to his father, for the old gentleman holds that cylinder as one of his choicest possessions on earth. (*Phonograph* 1900:143–44)

If the personal past could be partially recovered in the form of a sound recording, so, too, could the national historical past; the concept of "oral history" is almost as old as the process of technical sound recording itself, resulting in both commercial and instantaneous "home" cylinders preserving voices of famous statesmen and other public figures, as well as personal accounts of significant historical events. In 1904, a Mansfield, Ohio, phonograph dealer conceived the idea of playing a medley of Civil War marches for an aging veteran, and documenting the result in advertising copy, assuring readers that the account "is not in the least overdrawn. He actually wept, prayed, and swore."

Ah! You should see the old warrior's nostrils dilate and his eyes take on the fire of battle. The veteran is again back on the famous march from Atlanta to the sea. His arms swing and his feet beat to the inspiring rhythm of the song while his entire being is aquiver with the thrill which soldiers alone can feel. . . . Strange anomaly! Inexplicable paradox of the human soul: he weeps and great hot tears roll down the furrows which the years have laid into his cheeks. The heart of the rough old fighter is as tender as a maiden's. His lips again move with the prayers that were murmured before the charge, and then obvious [oblivious] to all present surroundings, carried forward in the irresistible current of the strife, he swears terrible oaths invoking the war god's vengeance upon the heads of his country's enemies. Was it real? Ask him.

In the brief period of ten or fifteen minutes the panorama of "The Great Rebellion," with all its sounds and sights, has passed before his eyes and filled his ears. Nay! More: He has been taken into it and lived it over again as he did in all its ghastly reality more than forty years ago.

The account ends with an alarming admonitory flourish:

> The Edison Phonograph, Mysterious of Sound, capable of portraying every passion of the human heart and every mood which can be made manifest to the human ear. Yet there are people who affect a dislike for this child of the brain of the "Wizard of Menlo Park." For them there can be but one verdict: A necrosed mentality, and atrophied soul; a being wholly animal in its selfishness and dead to every attribute that is noble. (*EPM* 2, no. 12 [1905]: 12)

The fountains of hyperbole that accompany advertisements for the phonograph were pragmatic at the immediate level: their purpose was increased sales. But the means to the goal—the vigorous mythologizing of the device and its inventor—was based on the market's responsiveness to such crypto-mystical imagery. The vision of "the Wizard of Menlo Park" both reinforced and reflected a popular attitude of reverence and admiration toward Edison, an attitude especially tenacious in small towns and rural areas where his commercial competitors had not actively competed for trade. In the late 1890s the Columbia Phonograph Company attempted to open new rural territory and adopted an opening line for its salesmen capitalizing on the patent controversy surrounding the development of the phonograph: "Did you know that Edison was not the inventor of the phonograph?" But the question provoked more fights than sales, and was quickly withdrawn (Read and Welch 1959:68). Though no Merlin, the Wizard of Menlo Park was accomplished in the practical arts most valued by his countrymen, and it was the phonograph, his favorite invention, that confirmed him in the role.

The advent of the phonograph offered the first medium by which men and women could mechanically document, frame, and evaluate sound events. This new capability offered profound implications throughout American society, from office to parlor, but its consequences were nowhere more profound than in the relatively new field of ethnography. First encounters with the phonograph inspired surprise, wariness, curiosity; the resolution of these emotions depended to a great degree on acquired attitudes concerning the causation, memory, identity, hearing, and the supernatural. Ethnographic field-workers and their subjects both brought these attitudes toward the phonograph to the ethnographic encounter, responding not only to one another but also to the machine—and to the strange new world of technocommunication announced by its raspy voice.

3

Collectors and the Phonograph

"Save, Save the Lore!"

> Give not, give not the yawning grave its plunder,
> Save, save the lore for future ages' joy:
> The stories full of beauty and of wonder
> The songs more pristine than the songs of Troy,
> The ancient speech forever to be banished—
> Lore that tomorrow to the grave goes down!
> All other thought from our horizon banish,
> Let any sacrifice our labor crown.
>
> *John Peabody Harrington[1]*

Academics get short shrift in the popular imagination, seldom glamorized, often ridiculed. In this regard, ethnographers can boast an image better than most. At a party, or in casual chat with an airplane seat partner, confessing "anthropology" or "folklore" as one's profession at least elicits the murmur, "How interesting—just like Margaret Mead," and we can boast at least one bona fide pop-culture hero, however spurious, in the person of archaeologist/anthropologist Indiana Jones. And if a cartoonist were to sketch the popular image of what we do, it would probably depict three emblematic elements: the fieldworker (earnest, intrepid but self-effacing, eager to "save the lore"), the subject (earnest, reflective, lore-laden), and a mechanical device mediating the encounter, the conduit for the exchange. The recorder as prop in this alluring mythic tableau is as much an acknowledged attribute of the stereotypical professional ethnographer as the doctor's stethoscope or the detective's magnifying glass. It is ironic, then, that historically it has been amateur collectors who have relied most enthusiastically on mechanical recording devices. From the time of its invention, though many professional anthropologists and folklorists used it, they most often disparaged its usefulness, understated their reliance on it, and often managed to avoid reference to its use in their formal work, although references abound in their notes, correspondences, and memoirs. In the official tableau favored by ethnographers during the phonograph era, its presence in the fieldwork encounter is airbrushed out of the picture—the ghost at the banquet. Only the surviving cylinders attest to the fact that phonograph recordings provided documentation for much of the most significant anthropological and folkloristic research from the time of its invention through the second decade of the century, continuing to prove their value even today.

It is unfortunate but perhaps appropriate that the individual credited with the first use of a recording machine should have been a poor candidate for a heroic professional tableau, with or without a mechanical prop. Emphatically not a swashbuckler, Jesse Walter Fewkes (1850–1930) was a proper Bostonian incapable of holding his seat on a horse, whose academic reputation rests on a series of monographs on Hopi ritual that his most sympathetic supporter dubbed "meticulously thorough, but soporific" (Lowie [1956] 1972:87).

Fewkes began his career as a zoologist, trained at Harvard and Leipzig, and affiliated himself with the renowned father-and-son naturalist team of Louis and Alexander Agassiz. His 1877 research project on marine invertebrates in California was supported by his wealthy Harvard classmate Augustus Hemenway, whose mother, Mary Hemenway, was a formidable philanthropic force in her own right. The previous year she had established the Hemenway Southwestern Archaeological Expedition under the direction of Frank Hamilton Cushing; with her encouragement Fewkes paid a visit to Zuni in the summer of 1890 (Swanton and Roberts 1931:609–16). According to his later account, it was in the course of this trip that the idea of using the phonograph as an ethnographic tool first took hold: "It occurred to me that I might employ the phonograph or graphophone as a means of recording the Zuni music. I had heard the same

Figure 3.1. Jesse Walter Fewkes. Courtesy of the Smithsonian Institution.

plan suggested by others, and have lately been informed that the idea of preserving Indian languages by the use of the phonograph had been in the minds of many ethnologists, but that they looked on this instrument, in its present condition, as too imperfect to be of value" (Fewkes 1891:55).[2]

Fired with the possibilities presented by the machine, Fewkes first traveled to Calais, Maine, in March 1890 to experiment with its use in a genuine field encounter. The Passamaquoddy recordings made by

Fewkes that represent our first ethnographic cylinder recordings were little more than a trial of the machine using a tribe located in relatively convenient proximity to Fewkes's Boston home. The result of his trip was a small but impressive collection of approximately thirty cylinders, the quality of which was good enough to lend itself to a valued native translation nearly a century later. Fewkes was intensely optimistic concerning the welcome the machine would find among those studying Indian culture, especially language: "It is a most valuable auxiliary in linguistic researches and . . . it should be used in the study of fast disappearing languages of races, and in making records of those which are rapidly becoming extinct. . . . The use of the phonograph among the Passamaquoddy has convinced me that the main characteristics of their language can be recorded and permanently preserved, either for study or demonstration, with this instrument" (Fewkes 1890d:268–69).

Fewkes's initial enthusiasm for the machine's use in the field had its basis in his training as a zoologist. In the article announcing the success of his experimental Passamaquoddy expedition in *Science* in May 1890, just two months after the Calais expedition, he observes, "What specimens are to the naturalist in describing genera and species, or what sections are to the histologist in the study of the cellular structure, the cylinders are to the study of language" (Fewkes 1890c:268). Conceptualizing cylinders as units of data fit compatibly with Fewkes's scientific training; it also provided a useful index of productivity to display to his benefactor. Mary Hemenway, like most of the philanthropic supporters of early ethnographic expeditions, was an enthusiastic collector of art and objects of historical interest accumulated in her travels, the product of an era notable for its "trophy mentality" toward material items as indices to success: financial, military, or social (Bronner 1986:9–10, 31). Fewkes lost no time in industriously publicizing the success of his initial Passamaquoddy foray to the scientific community as extensively as possible, signaling his intention to try the phonograph as soon as possible under the more demanding conditions at Zuni (Fewkes 1890b, 1890c, 1890d).

Meanwhile, Cushing, the incumbent director of the Hemenway

Expedition in Zuni, was hospitalized in Washington, D.C., and *hors de combat*—a situation that presented possibilities for Fewkes. Poor Cushing was desperate to return to work and resume his interrupted relationship with the people of Zuni and his role as director of the Hemenway Expedition—desperate enough, indeed, to take comfort from the prediction of a professional psychic that he would do so. But institutional pull prevailed over prognostication: Mary Hemenway removed the ailing Cushing from his position in the summer of 1890, replacing him with Fewkes for the remaining four years of the project (Hinsley 1983:61).

Fewkes paraded his subsequent efforts with the phonograph in the Southwest in a heated profusion of articles (Fewkes 1890a, 1890b, 1890c, 1890d, 1891). Nevertheless, his interest in the phonograph, and indeed his interest in the study of living Indian culture, waned after the death of Mrs. Hemenway in 1894. In the following year he moved from Cambridge to Washington, D.C., and assumed a position as staff ethnologist at the Bureau of American Ethnology, where his interests and activities were mostly archaeological. He became chief of the Bureau of American Ethnology in 1918, remaining there until his retirement in 1928 (Swanton and Roberts 1931:616). He is not known to have made any ethnographic recordings using the phonograph after 1891.

Fewkes's activities in Maine, Boston, and New Mexico in 1890 remain the earliest systematically documented and published instances of the ethnographic use of the phonograph. Cylinders from these sessions survive, as do the rather self-congratulatory publications attesting to the pioneering nature of this work. There is, however, tantalizing evidence that in his use of the phonograph he may have been preceded by his brilliant and intuitive rival, Frank Hamilton Cushing (1857–1900)—a far more charismatic candidate for the tableau of ethnologist-as-hero. It would be both ironic and fitting if he were also the first ethnologist purposely to efface the image of the phonograph from the picture.

Captain John G. Bourke, one of the earliest members of the American Folklore Society and an active collector himself, noted in his

Figure 3.2. Frank Hamilton Cushing in Zuni dress. Courtesy of the Smithsonian Institution.

journal for the date May 26, 1889, a visit to the hospitalized Cushing, accompanied by his four-year-old daughter, Sara. According to Bourke, "Cushing had a graphophone from which he extracted the words of Zuni, Apache, and Navajo dances, to Sara's undisguised horror and astonishment" (Bloom 1936:204; see also Brandes 1965:153). If Bourke can be relied upon, then Cushing had ethnographic recordings in his possession about a year before Fewkes began experimenting with the phonograph.

It is possible that Cushing himself both performed and recorded the mysterious cylinders that appalled little Miss Bourke; his identification with Zuni culture in particular was intense, and he had in fact beguiled the imagination and subsequently the patronage of Mrs. Hemenway with parlor renditions of native folktales when courting her support of the expedition in the early 1880s (Mark 1980:107). But it would also be typical of Cushing to have made recordings of Indian languages in the field but never publicize them, leaving no account of the matter. Franz Boas once praised Cushing as "an exceedingly able man." After a pause, he dryly appended, "I'm afraid his work will have to be done all over again" (Lowie [1956] 1972:79–80). Even aside from his notorious disorganization and lack of system in maintaining fieldnotes, it could be argued that the creation of a body of discrete documentary cultural "items" was not his style—too cold, too particularized, too dispassionate and disengaged from the subject— too much that of the naturalist in search of specimens.

Today's historians of the early years of ethnology find it easy to target the unsympathetic Fewkes and to valorize the glamorous Cushing, whose very flaws and excesses had an attractive panache. Cushing immersed himself in every aspect of pueblo life, convinced that each expressive form from foodways to folktale conveyed some facet of a coherent cultural system, while Fewkes supped on SS Peirce canned goods sent from Boston by Mrs. Hemenway and engaged in insular institutional and professional infighting with colleagues on site. Cushing labored earnestly to move from English to broken Spanish to yet more broken Zuni, achieving at last a "strangely complicated tongue, [spoken] not perfectly but fluently and easily" (Hinsley 1983:57), while Fewkes mechanically recorded language and ceremony but learned neither Spanish nor Zuni, documenting his collecting with the assistance of the phonograph—a pioneering strategy that anthropologist and historian Curtis Hinsley ironically characterizes as "an advance in technology, but possibly a retreat from understanding" (63). Although considered affable by his colleagues in Boston and Washington, Fewkes was not regarded with respect by his colleagues in the field. We read with mild embarrassment the vignettes of Fewkes's fieldwork recorded by his many contemporary detractors:

the stereotypical city slicker who never quite got down and dirty, unless you count the dusty results of his unfortunate encounter with a recalcitrant Zuni pony. On the other hand, the photos of Cushing posed in the trappings of the Priesthood of the Bow inspire a smile, accompanied by an indulgent sigh at the naiveté of his proud presumption—in our hearts envying that elusive gift of rapport that he appeared to have had in abundance.

The figure of Cushing—resplendent in his regalia, without the intrusive distraction of the phonograph—represents an alternative mythic tableau to the triad of collector/informant/machine, a vision in which the mechanics of documentation become magically, ziplessly, transparent. An advocate of what he termed "the reciprocal method" of ethnography, his sessions with Zunis and others were based on an informal process of cultural exchange in which Cushing offered folktales and myths of European origin in response to those of his hosts (Mark 1980:103). As a prototype—and a bit more—of the participant observer, Cushing can be seen as the precursor of the seductive later epistemologies in which the demarcation between the roles of investigator and subject begins to blur, finally evaporating altogether in recent works in which the investigator *becomes* the subject, the investigation of culture represented as a mere stimulant to self-discovery and self-revelation (Jackson 1989; O'Meara 1990).

Although outsiders envision their mythic ethnologist with recording device in hand, most past and present ethnographers do not—unless, like most folklorists, they are specifically committed to examination of particular expressive forms such as song or narrative, in which verbatim texts are essential. In his examination of Fewkes and Cushing, Curtis Hinsley introduces the image of the "marbling" or "bronzing" of the American Indian as part of a process of artistic abstraction that, while it claims to ennoble, in fact serves to freeze a living world in metal and stone. In some instances, the reticence of early collectors concerning their use of mechanical means of recording perhaps represented an implicit resistance to the "waxing" of their relationship with native informants and the products of that relationship—through the reduction of the fieldwork encounter from a dramatic human interaction accomplished through skill and rapport to a mechanical transaction accomplished by a mere flip of a lever. Making conspicuous use of the machine and reporting on its use attracted attention to the inevitable artificiality of the encounter. Early investigators drew their professional audience's gaze away from this artificiality by drawing a veil of invisibility over the presence of the ethnographer altogether. Later fieldworkers evaded the issue by framing their role as what Morris Freilich termed "marginal natives." In neither case did the phonograph fit the picture. In the inevitable fieldwork dilemma—the tug between personal attraction to the culture at hand and the rewards anticipated from the academic culture to which the fieldworker would return—the phonograph figured rather too evidently on the side of "profitability" over "sociability."[3] This appears to have been the case with Cushing, whose discomfort with the pressure that professional requirements placed on his personal relationship with the Zuni community only increased as his grip on the Hemenway Project directorship loosened.

Even more important a factor in the invisibility of the phonograph in formal accounts was the perception that a truly scientific record required a thorough purging of the messy means by which information was acquired. In most publications of those individuals whose cylinder recordings survive today, it is difficult to uncover means by which the data was collected. For reasons both disciplinary and political, in the early years of the century the journal of choice for professional ethnographers publishing text-based research was the *Journal of American Folk-Lore* (later "Folklore"; Zumwalt 1988:31, 68–69). Between 1890 and 1935, the years in which the phonograph was in extensive use as an ethnographic tool, some 485 instances occur in *JAF* in which full texts were presented in a typographical style indicating that they were complete, presumably verbatim transcriptions of material collected in the field. Out of these, 384 make no mention whatsoever of the circumstances under which the texts were taken down, whether by pencil in English from a translator, by pencil in a phonetic rendering later translated, or by phonograph. In fact, only twelve articles throughout this entire period mention the phonograph at all, although external evidence demonstrates that members of the society were using it regularly. Existing references to the collecting process are couched in ambiguous terms: the material was "communicated," "obtained," "secured," "taken down," "taken from the lips of," or merely "heard." In general, discussions of the use of the phonograph were either published in articles concerned specifically with method and procedure, or were shared informally in published or unpublished correspondence and memoirs.

The phonograph is mentioned most frequently in the early issues of the *Journal of American Folk-Lore* not in articles but rather in a regular feature titled "Local Meetings and Other Notices," which chronicled the regional gatherings of Society members. In these elegantly chatty accounts, as much social as professional in tone, the phonograph finally emerges from the shadows into unself-conscious period vignettes that reveal much concerning underlying attitudes and assumptions of participants. On February 15, 1892, the Boston Association of the American Folk-Lore Society met at the home of philanthropist Mary Hemenway, whose protegé, Fewkes, spoke on Zuni religion. "To illustrate the locality and the ritual processions, photographs were exhibited with the lantern, while the sacred songs were reproduced by the graphophone. . . . A large attendance was present, and the remarkable character of the exposition was recognized" ("Local Meetings" 1892:158). Washington Matthews addressed the seventeen charter members of the Baltimore branch of the Society on the occasion of their first meeting in 1894, illustrating his presentation with examples of Navajo songs played on a phonograph. With the efficiency of the machine as an ethnographic tool demonstrated, he emphasized to these new members the importance of swift and thorough ethnographic investigation, observing that "the study of folklore did not resemble the natural sciences, which might be left to natural and gradual development, but must be taken up at once. . . . Education and civilization were destroying the material, and the longer the delay the less complete would be the understanding of the subject" ("Local Meetings" 1895:90–91). A note concerning the proceedings of the Boston Branch of the Society on December 17, 1897, relates that "Miss Alice Fletcher, of Washington…spoke on the topic of Indian Songs, and stated that much she would say was based on the thousand or more phonographic records of this wild music which she had gathered among the Indians themselves. . . . Miss Fletcher's paper gave a clear idea of Indian song, and at its close Mrs. Matthews with the voice, and Mr. Clement Bouvé on the violoncello, rendered several examples of this weird music" ("Local Meetings" 1898:79).

The invisibility of the phonograph in formal, professional settings extended to both mechanical and human facilitators of fieldwork. The Bureau of American Ethnology was devoted entirely to gathering of data concerning Indian culture in the United States, and its staff and consultants used the phonograph extensively in their wide-ranging efforts. Yet mentions of the phonograph are relatively scant and unelaborated in the publications of the BAE, despite the fact that thousands of cylinder recordings were made under this agency's auspices, and no indication of these holdings appear in its annual inventories.[4] Wax cylinder records themselves were valued only as a means to derive written transcriptions in phonetic orthography, English textual translations, or musical transcriptions in standard notation more easily from the collected material (Brady et al. 1984:9). It was these "derived texts," not the cylinders themselves, that represented the primary basis for descriptive and analytical work in folklore and anthropology. Consequently, the wax cylinders containing recordings of songs and narratives seem to have been considered hardly more important than steno pads once a letter has been typed in its final form. The cylinders were often discarded; the texts derived from them were subject to modification according to the needs, taste, ideology, or whim of the transcriber.

Uninhibited references to textual alterations abound in the early issues of the *Journal of American Folk-Lore*. Clara Kern Bayliss even felt obliged to inform the reader that the texts published in her article "Philippine Folk-Tales" were *occasionally* verbatim: "In these legends, in a few instances, the exact phrases of the narrators have been retained for the sake of their quaintness" (1908:46n). A certain amount of freedom with the text was expected, particularly from those not involved with linguistic research but rather concerned with the areas of myth, ritual, and narrative. As D. Demetraeapoulou and Cora DuBois remarked, "a linguist records a text verbatim, whereas an ethnographer may not" (1932:381). The preference for "derived texts" was not merely an aesthetic choice favoring prettified material over raw, nor was it a purely expedient choice based on the convenience, familiarity, and conventional authority of the written over the aural. Rather, the choice resulted from an attitude toward texts themselves in which particular performances were important only insofar as they could be used to reconstruct a paradigm for song, story, narrative, or myth in a given culture.

It was this emphasis on the paradigmatic over the specific, and not necessarily methodological ignorance or negligence that led to a de-emphasis of the particulars of fieldwork episodes and encounters and a concomitant editorial freedom on the part of collectors in the alteration of material from a verbatim form. Even Fewkes, pioneer of the use of the phonograph in the field, virtually took for granted the necessity of improving the material so collected: "The phonograph records the story exactly as the Indian tells it; and although free translation of it may, and probably must be made, to render the story comprehensible, we can always preserve the phonographic record as a check on exaggeration, or as a reference in critical discussion of the subject matter of the story. In this way the phonograph imparts to the study of folk-lore, as far as the aborigines are concerned, a scientific basis which it had not previously had, and makes approximately accurate" (Fewkes 1890c:268).

A few scholars such as Percy Grainger and Benjamin Ives Gilman delighted in the opportunity offered by the phonograph to study specific performances in detail. But they were the exception: Grainger's meticulous transcriptions of individual performances were dismissed by Ralph Vaughan Williams as "mad" and "a waste of time"—"as a singer would make alterations to a tune with each performance, there was little point in making a detailed transcription of a single performance" (Yates 1982:274). Far more typical were the sentiments of

John Comfort Fillmore, who sought to determine what "the Indian" *meant* to sing and the extent to which this generic character succeeded. Most fieldworkers who chose to use the phonograph generally did not do so with the objective of securing and preserving a perfectly faithful verbatim or note-perfect rendition of a single performance. The norm of word-for-word publication of texts, "warts and all," derives from the exigencies of much more recent research trends such as ethnopoetics, performance theory, and others in folklore and anthropology.

Even in recent years, when ethnographic conventions concerning presentation of text have become more stringent, the actual process by which such texts are acquired often remains obscure. Writing in the 1970s, Inta Carpenter in folklore and Morris Freilich in anthropology both noted the persistence of a stubborn reticence with regard to procedure in the publication of the results of field research up to that time, suggesting that this methodological obscurity reflected a vision of the pursuit of data in the field as a kind of rite of passage, in which the "initiate" was reluctant to reveal the mysteries and to put on public display the many methodological compromises that fieldwork situations demand. "Only the conclusions matter anyway, is the standard motto" (Carpenter 1978:205; Freilich 1970:14). At the time Carpenter and Freilich wrote, however, the conventions of ethnography were undergoing profound changes resulting in the emergence of self-consciousness—the presence of the investigator—in the written results of research. This phenomenon was examined in its historical context in a landmark article by Dennison Nash and Ronald Wintrob (1972), in which they attribute the shift toward a more direct voice on the part of the ethnologist-author to social change within the discipline of anthropology, and alterations in the global politics affecting the attitude of "subject" cultures. But the change in conventions of ethnography pertained largely to the extent to which an investigator was forthcoming about "transactional processes between the ethnographer and his subjects [and] of his own positive and negative reactions during fieldwork" (527)—questions concerning emotional affect, bias, and relationship—rather than consistent revelation of literal methods of fieldwork, which remain elusive in ethnographic publication to this day. We may now participate indirectly in the researchers' most intimate and visceral exchanges in the field. We enjoy voyeur status at petting sessions with spirit beings, try to still our queasy stomachs at intentionally nauseating descriptions of native cuisine, and not only observe sacred ritual but observe the observer converted and cured. The scenes are evoked with vivid sensory immediacy, the taste offered waferlike on our waiting tongues. But we don't necessarily know any more about the quotidian nuts and bolts of data gathering that made possible these compelling evocations. Self-consciousness in ethnography remains a highly selective process.

The roots of this selectivity lie in the conventions of "realist" ethnography as it took shape in the early years of this century, in which the experiential authority of the writer was conveyed by an omniscient voice rather like that of God in medieval mystery plays, heard but never seen, identifying and interpreting "typical" behaviors and expressive forms within the subject culture. In his salient typology of ethnographic writing, *Tales of the Field*, John Van Maanen notes the characteristic emphasis of the "typical" rather than the "specific" in realist writings: "little is told about the particular experiences of the people studied, but much about the categories or institutions that are said to order their lives" (1988:48). The realist legacy minimizes the practical specifics of the fieldwork encounter, often so inconveniently artificial and contrived, in order to maintain the carefully constructed authority of the writer, privileging the paradigmatic over the particular except where specific observed detail enhances the impression of authority based on experience.

During the period in which the conventions of realist ethnography emerged, no ethnographer was more engaged by the dilemma of the paradigmatic versus the particular in presentation of fieldwork, and the issue of experiential authority, than Franz Boas, whose paternal relationship to the nascent discipline of anthropology is summarized affectionately in the nickname given to him by his students: "Papa Franz." Like Fewkes, a scientist by training, with Cushing he shared a deeply humanistic worldview (Hinsley 1983:68). The comprehension of these apparent oppositions in one individual is perhaps understood in light of the German tradition of a scientific training not necessarily divorced from expressive, aesthetic, and even Romantic concerns. Boas's work and teaching was characterized by a naturalist's attraction to text-based fieldwork collection; the body of work has been criticized by subsequent generations of scholars as more accumulative than evaluative—driven as a fieldworker, he was deeply reluctant to theorize in advance of his data, and that mountain of data never achieved the critical mass he seems to have required to pronounce beyond his firm conviction in favor of diffusion as the dominant factor in cross-cultural expressive forms.

From the turn of the century through the early thirties, most of the professional folklorists using the phonograph as a fieldwork tool were directly influenced in doing so by Franz Boas. Their use of the machine effectively fulfilled Boas's mandate to pursue "folklore"— that is "people['s] records of themselves in their own words" (Reichard 1943:55). The results of their investigations in this area were most frequently published in the *Journal of American Folk-Lore*, which by 1908 the "Boasians" had effectively commandeered and would control for almost thirty years, edited by Boas himself (1908–1924), Ruth Benedict (1925–1939), and Gladys Reichard (1940) (Zumwalt 1988:31–32). Such a mandate led many of Boas's colleagues and students, folklorists and anthropologists, to supplement their notebook and pencil with a phonograph in the field; Gladys Reichard, Paul Radin, Ruth Underhill, Clark Wissler, Robert H. Lowie, Helen Heffron Roberts, Martha Beckwith, Elsie Clews Parsons, and Alfred Kroeber among others all made significant cylinder recordings of field data. The reasons for this consistent methodological pattern are rooted in the emergent culture of anthropology at Columbia, including elements of ideology and an intellectual zeitgeist as well as more practical persuasions.

Use of the phonograph satisfied the passionate urgency conveyed by Boas to his colleagues and students. Total immersion in a culture as a technique demands expertise, time, and interpersonal skills of a high order. Although Boas's fieldwork did tend at times toward what would later be called "participant observation" of general social patterns, the basis for his fieldwork was emphatically on collection of *texts* (Stocking 1974:85). Verbatim textual transcription is exhausting for ethnographer, translator, and informant. With a phonograph, a collector could gather many times the quantity of linguistic and musical material possible using other means. Theodora Kroeber described her husband Alfred's experience with Boas as a teacher at Columbia at the turn of the century in terms he himself must have provided, since it was long before their meeting and marriage:

> Virgin but fleeting—this was the urgency and the poetry of Boas' message. Everywhere over the land were virgin languages, brought to their polished and idiosyncratic perfection of grammar and syntax without benefit of a single recording scratch of stylus on papyrus or stone; living languages orally learned and transmitted and about to die with their last speakers. Everywhere there were to be discovered Ways of Life, many many ways. There were gods and created worlds unlike other gods and worlds, with extended relationships and values and ideals and dreams unlike anything known or imagined elsewhere, all soon to be forever lost—part of the human condition, part of the beautiful heartbreaking history of man. The time was late, the dark forces of invasion had almost done their ignorant work of annihilation. To the field then! With notebook and pencil, record, record, record. (Kroeber 1970:51)

One might add "the phonograph" to "notebook and pencil." The importance of efficiency in field collecting and the usefulness of the phonograph in boosting productivity emerges with special clarity when one considers that, by today's standards, field trips were normally quite short during most of the cylinder era, seldom lasting longer than a couple of months at a time, and sometimes as brief as a mere day or two. Boas and his students, though considered quintessential fieldworkers, did not spend extended periods in the field in general—certainly not on the scale of later British anthropologists following the Malinowskian tradition. Rosalie H. Wax has pointed out that the nature of funding of early ethnographic work did not allow for long periods in the field, and in fact the nature of their data did not require it. They seldom achieved full fluency in the native languages, relying heavily on bilingual interpreters and informants. Boas himself made thirteen trips to the Northwest Coast, seldom spending more than two months at a time, and seems to have "worked" at least forty culture areas (Wax 1971:31–32). The phonograph, for all its limitation, was a valuable tool in responding to the evangelical call to "record."

There may have been an ideological, even theoretical appeal to the use of the phonograph as well. Although Boas himself did not go as far as influential physicist Ernst Mach in adopting a pragmatic view of scientific laws as purely heuristic and potentially temporary constructs (Stocking 1974:11), there is nonetheless in his anthropological work and teachings more than a whiff of Mach's radical sensationalist epistemology—the notion that knowledge must be rooted not in speculation but in experience, unimpeded by externally imposed paradigms and categories. The Machian epistemological revolution and the accompanying redefinition of knowledge in the wake of Charles Sanders Peirce's pragmaticism (especially the more diffuse interpretation and application found in William James's construct) can be seen in Boas's insistence on fieldwork incorporating direct observation and documentation of specific expressive forms; perhaps as well these intellectual trends exerted a negative influence affecting Boas's notorious reluctance to move beyond collection of texts to more expansive and theoretical works synthesizing the materials collected.[5]

There is a clear relationship between the critical positivism espoused by followers of Mach in many disciplines and the anthropological notion of cultural relativism pursued by Boas and his colleagues with missionary zeal: "We learn from the data of ethnology that not only our ability and knowledge but also the manner and ways of our feeling and thinking is the result of our upbringing as individuals and our history as a people. To draw conclusions about the development of mankind as a whole we must try to divest ourselves of these influences, and this is only possible by immersing ourselves in the spirit of primitive peoples whose perspectives and development have almost nothing in common with our own" (Boas [1889a] 1974:71). The relationship with Mach is largely implicit in Boas's writing and teaching but becomes explicit in the work and activity of students and co-workers such as Robert Lowie, Paul Radin, and Elsie Clews Parsons (Deacon 1997:100–107).

But the very process of "immersion in the spirit" of peoples whose perspectives and development are utterly foreign is fraught with the risk of unconscious superimposition of the investigator's own native categories and constructs. The risk is greatest when the attempt is made at the most abstract and inclusive levels, as in the willy-nilly categorization of societies along an evolutionary continuum from "savagery" to "civilization" against which Boas campaigned so vigorously. The risk persists in the process of recording the most basic expressive forms, even inhering in the cross-cultural perception of as irreducible a form as linguistic phonemes. In an 1889 essay titled "On Alternating Sounds," Boas observes that fieldnotes even of scientists trained in supposedly objective systems for recording language demonstrate patterns of error—"mishearing"—consistent with their native tongue: "the nationality even of well-trained observers may readily be recognized" (Boas [1889b] 1974:75).

The spirit of critical positivism energizing the American anthropologists clustered around Boas—the so-called Columbia school—supported the extensive use of the phonograph among the members of the group. It provided a form of documentation directly apprehensible to the senses, presumably uncontaminated by the observer's inevitable categorical and perceptual biases. Boas himself had experimented extensively with the phonograph in 1893 and 1895, recording Kwakiutl and Thompson River Indian material (Boas 1925:319, Lee 1984a:viii); while not effusive concerning the experience, he continued to use the device intermittently throughout his career.[6]

Finally, there may be a practical and human reason for the attraction of the device for this group. "Critical positivism" was a thrilling approach to ethnology for neophyte Columbia anthropologists when the topic was on the agenda in the familiar intellectual give-and-take of Alexander Goldenweiser's discussion group, the now-celebrated Pearson Circle.[7] It was in this stimulating and urbane setting that Lowie and Radin in particular first grappled with the implications of the "new science" for anthropology. But the implementation of these insights in fieldwork represented a challenge of a different order. The "how-to" component in anthropological education at Columbia in the early years of the century was notably lacking. Papa Franz was a vigorous supporter of his students, but his pedagogy was notoriously unspecific; Boas's teaching style in this regard has been generously described by Herskovits as "subtle," more bluntly by Lowie as "odd" (Herskovits 1973:22; Lowie 1959:3).[8] Use of the phonograph created a body of data supposedly pure in Machian terms; it also supplied a welcome degree of practical concreteness to the methodological problems posed by implementation of Boas's anthropological agenda. For insecure beginners in the field, armed only with the memory of Boas's lectures on linguistics and statistics, the phonograph provided a welcome focus and distraction as they found their feet.

They used the machine, but most of the Columbia ethnographers never overcame a certain ambivalence, even hostility, toward it, even after some of the technical shortcomings of the machine had been resolved and its price brought within their range. Granted, the phonograph was only suitable for the documentation of certain kinds of cultural phenomena: it was blind to nonverbal aspects of ritual and manifestations of material culture, as well as to intangible behavioral patterns such as kinship and social structure. The use of the phonograph automatically framed information as a presentation or performance, something set aside and special: brief, powerful, and permanent. As such it was best suited to record materials that were naturally and intrinsically "performances," formulaically defined and set off in the normal course of events from the usual flow of social expression—that is, songs, religious ceremonies, and narratives. But it was precisely these expressive forms that were of particular interest to ethnologists of the Boasian tribe; the source of their ambivalence must be sought elsewhere.

Folklorist Simon Bronner has characterized the late nineteenth and early twentieth century as a period in American intellectual history in the course of which examination of "time" and "space" in the sciences became professionalized: "Geographers and naturalists offered more exact descriptions of space, historians and geologists gave them for time" (Bronner 1986:55). Ethnologists faced a more difficult dilemma: quantification of space and time in the arena of culture and tradition posed a challenge to both method and theory—a challenge to both scientific accuracy and humanistic values. The phonograph seemingly represented a useful if not ideal tool in this process of professionalization: it captured sound events objectively and with some degree of fidelity. Although cumbersome to pack into remote areas, it was not a significant burden in an era when even those travelers "roughing it" thought nothing of carrying with them an extraordinary amount of gear by today's standards. More burdensome than the literal encumbrance of the phonograph was the symbolic baggage that accompanied its use. Though it could be seen as a gleaming modern emblem of professionalization of ethnology—Fewkes certainly regarded it as such—its presence in the fieldwork encounter could also imply a deficit on the part of the ethnographer: lack of full linguistic fluency, lack of training enabling swift and accurate linguistic or musical transcription, or, most damning of all, lack of the easy and full identification with the subjects that would lend fullest possible authority to the ethnographer's accounts. Its mechanical nature, at first glance an asset in the "measurement" of data representing cultural time and space, may have seemed uncomfortably reminiscent of inappropriate tools such as the calipers used for measurement of cranial capacity early in the careers of ethnographers such as Boas, Wissler, Lowie, and Kroeber, later to be recalled by some with regret. As a result, the relatively few evaluations of the usefulness of the phonograph surviving from the period suggest an ambivalence on the part of fieldworkers toward its usefulness that cannot be fully explained by its technical limitations or practicality.

For example, Paul Radin's eighty-seven cylinder recordings made of Winnebago material in 1908 represent the earliest mechanically documented data available from that tribe, a significant and admirable accomplishment. Yet in reflecting some years later on the fieldwork of this period he underplayed the use of the machine, suggesting that, except for a few songs, he used the phonograph "sparingly," favoring instead either direct dictation or obtaining texts set down by the informants themselves in a syllabary adapted from that of the Sauk and Fox:

> In 1908, when only the old Edison phonograph was known, this method had too many manifest drawbacks to warrant its use for anything but music. A text obtained in this fashion in 1908, one might suppose, and I did so suppose, would be markedly inferior to one procured in the two ways I have mentioned. However, this proved definitely not to be the case. The narratives recorded on the Edison phonograph cylinders were given by the best of my early informants, Charles Houghton. The circumstances were exceptionally unfavorable. I could use only the small cylinders and it must have been apparent to Houghton that I was in a great hurry. Yet, when compared with the narratives that Houghton had dictated to me directly, there was no evidence that this procedure, utterly new to him, had any perceptible effect on him. The style of narration, a highly individualistic one, differs, in no respect, from that found in Houghton's dictated texts. (Radin 1949:5)

Curiously, Radin concludes from this reluctant experiment that all of the methods he chose—dictation by hand, transcription by the informant in syllabary, and recording with the phonograph—have *equal* merit. The disadvantages of the phonograph alluded to by Radin must have been a matter of inconvenience and perhaps his own discomfort with the device, since its performance was impeccable. Would Houghton have expressed a preference for the phonograph if consulted?

Similarly, ethnomusicologist Helen Heffron Roberts, a later student of Boas, made superbly effective use of the cylinder phonograph, notably in her collection of Northern California Karok and Konomihu music. These recordings represent possibly the finest single cylinder collection in the Archive of Folk Culture: technically high in quality and supported by splendidly accurate transcriptions and documentation. Her commitment to the cylinder phonograph as a tool led her to investigate the technical side of recording as well, consulting with Edison himself concerning problems of preservation and rerecording cylinders (Roberts and Lachmann 1935). Yet she too expressed reservations concerning the use of the phonograph:

Longhand notation is, of course, very much slower than record making and requires patience in all concerned. On the other hand, it has many merits. It affords excellent opportunities to the [collector] for observing the musical intelligence and ability of the singer, his variability in repetition to repetition in melody, form, text, etc., as would not be noted under the rather more strenuous and rapid recordings by the phonograph. It also affords an excellent chance for conversation by the way, for questions bound to arise which would never occur to the collector in the more perfunctory process of making records, and would only too late be put by the transcriber. Moreover, in this more leisurely pursuit, an informant may appeal to a bystander for assistance in recollecting, or arguments may arise which, to the alert collector, may furnish valuable additional data. Longhand notation is the best method possible for checking on impromptu composing and frauds. Phonograph records and longhand notations of the same song may be compared with advantage. (Roberts 1931:57–58)

Although the limitations of the phonograph were real, some of the difficulty experienced by ethnographers such as Radin and Roberts may not have related to the workings of the machine itself but instead to their adjustment to an unfamiliar process of documentation in which the oral nature of their material was retained rather than immediately reduced to written form. The historically shaped sensorium of ethnographers of the period was still essentially a post-Enlightenment environment in which meaningful sound was automatically spatialized—and specialized—in the form of the written word. In Walter Ong's terms, their frame of reference was fully "chirographic," centered on the preeminence of visual evidence, and the authority of text (1967:87–88, 1982:136). The contemporary era characterized by Ong as that of "secondary orality," in which the voice becomes newly alive and significant through electronic media, was being ushered in by the invention of the very machine the early ethnographers used with such obvious reluctance. Some of their hesitation may have had less to do with the limitations of the machine itself than with adjustment to an unfamiliar process of documentation in which the oral nature of their material was retained indefinitely, instead of being immediately reduced to written form. Despite their success with the phonograph, Radin and Roberts obviously hesitated to endorse it unreservedly as a tool—an attitude typical of Boas's students, reflecting both their experience and the opinion of Papa Franz himself.

Boas's influence on the course of ethnography, and the attention this influence indirectly drew to the usefulness of mechanical means of recording, predated and extended well beyond his circle of colleagues and students at Columbia. By the turn of the century, he had already systematically developed his agenda for the professionalization of American anthropology in ways that promoted the use of the phonograph in government-sponsored fieldwork. As early as 1887, he had corresponded with John Wesley Powell, director and founder of the Bureau of American Ethnology, concerning the publication of his first ethnological research in the Baffin Islands. By the early 1890s, he was fully engaged in the Byzantine politics of the organization and was offered a position directing editorial work for the Bureau (Stocking 1974:59–60; 1992:64–68). Although he turned down this offer, he benefited from the agency throughout the nineties in ways that he could not from other more archaeologically oriented museums and institutions. The BAE indirectly subsidized his work on linguistics and mythology by purchasing his manuscripts and fieldnotes at a generous price. For his part, he did not hesitate to express his views concerning administration and policy both to Powell and to Samuel Langley, head of the Smithsonian Institution, of which the BAE was a part. In the course of Boas's prolonged "systematic self-professionalization" as an anthropologist, he had concluded that the growth of the field and the future of the BAE required that "those lines of human activity that do *not* find expression in material objects—namely language, thought, customs, and I may add, anthropometric measurements—be investigated thoroughly and carefully," a conviction he impressed upon Langley in correspondence concerning a possible successor to Powell in 1893 (Hinsley 1981:251).[9]

Correspondence with Powell and his associate, William John McGee, in 1893 reveals Boas's early commitment to the essential importance of collection of full texts of cultural materials; we have seen that it was in this same year that he first experimented with the phonograph as an ethnographic tool. As the policy shift influenced by Boas drew the BAE collecting projects and publication initiatives ever more deeply into areas concerned with such nonmaterial aspects of culture as myth, music, narrative, and linguistics, the phonograph became an essential tool for the ethnographers employed by the BAE. As it happened, Powell retained control of the Bureau until his death in 1902, and although he was replaced by W. H. Holmes, no friend to Boas, the emphasis on nonmaterial forms of expression, especially linguistic and musical, remained strong. The Bureau publication of Boas's *Handbook of American Indian Languages* in 1911 bears witness to an influence that would continue for at least two more decades in the BAE's history (Stocking 1992:60–91).

At first glance, it is difficult to reconcile the connection between Franz Boas, champion of a relativistic approach to culture and enemy of imposed external schemata, and John Wesley Powell—so profoundly influenced by the evolutionary constructs of Lewis Morgan that a personal copy of the latter's work *Ancient Societies* was presented to each new employee of the Bureau (Resek 1960:150). Boas and Powell present a fascinating contrast: Boas the product of a richly textured and deeply rooted European intellectual synthesis of science and humanities, Powell the restless heir to generations of a very American type of military explorer-naturalists dating at least back to Meriwether Lewis. In a widely used text, anthropologist Marvin Harris ungraciously dismisses Powell as a "hayseed and a bumpkin," adding that in comparison with Boas, he was "a distressingly undisciplined dabbler." Curtis Hinsley characterizes the Bureau under Powell's direction as the embodiment of "a concept of scientific anthropology that became a historical reject, a road not taken in the professional development of American anthropology" (1976:37–38). It is true that Powell and his staff were often less than theoretically rigorous and their embrace of evolutionist constructs with their accompanying ethnocentric and racist assumptions were incompatible with attitudes accepted in today's ethnographic disciplines—attitudes shaped in part by the efforts and influence of Boas. But Powell was the best-known ethnologist of his era, and his grip on the purse strings that controlled federally funded ethnographic efforts during his tenure at the BAE was firm and sure at a time when Boas was still making an uneasy transition from geographic determinism to a more broadly based study of culture. What Powell and Boas shared in abundance was their orientation toward the *past*—a preoccupation in their ethnological work that may have had roots in their previous training in geography and geology, studies that predisposed them to look for artifactual evidence for their historical speculations, whether in the form of a geological specimen, a pot shard, or a song text recorded in wax.[10]

Indeed, the BAE's roots lay in federal geological and geographical survey work undertaken in the 1870s. A veteran of the Union Army who had lost an arm at the battle of Shiloh, Major Powell began his civilian career as director of these expeditions. According to Powell's final report to the Department of the Interior in 1877, the work included "classification of Indian tribes, such classification being not only of scientific interest, but of great importance in the administration of Indian affairs" (Judd 1967:5), which suggests his awareness of the potential political and administrative applications of work he would later support as head of the Bureau. As a result of his initiative, the agency was founded in 1879 as the Bureau of Ethnology, to be renamed the Bureau of American Ethnology in 1894.

Powell's admiration for the work of Lewis Henry Morgan definitively shaped the early years of the BAE. He described Morgan's firsthand observations of Iroquois life in *League of the Ho-de-no-sau-nee* as "the first scientific account of an Indian tribe ever given to the world" (Powell 1880:115), and took to heart Morgan's assertion in *Ancient Societies* that study of American Indian culture provided a unique window on the stages of the process of development undergone by all societies:

> When discovered, the American Indian tribes represented three distinct ethnical periods, and more completely than they were elsewhere then represented upon the earth. Materials for ethnology, philology, and archaeology were offered in unparalleled abundance, but as these sciences scarcely existed until the present century, and are but feebly prosecuted

among us at the present time, the workmen have been unequal to the work. Moreover, while the fossil remains buried in the earth will keep for the future student, the remains of Indian arts, languages, and institutions will not. They are perishing daily, and have been perishing for upwards of three centuries. The ethnic life of the Indian tribes is declining under the influence of American civilization, their arts and languages are disappearing, and their institutions are dissolving. After a few more years, facts that now may be gathered with ease will become impossible of discovery. The circumstances appeal strongly to Americans to enter this great field and gather its abundant harvest. (Morgan 1877:vii–viii)

Intrinsic to Morgan's approach to ethnology and archaeology was the value of the artifact—the physical object that would provide the clue to the level of technical development of a people, and hence indicate the stage of their progress toward "civilization." Consequently, the BAE fieldworkers were intensely *thing*-oriented—an attitude shared and encouraged by their parent agency, the Smithsonian. The prevalent nineteenth-century vision of a museum was a place where a variety of interesting and unique objects might be stored—a kind of scientific omnium-gatherum (Hinsley 1981:64–77). This item-centered attitude carried over into aspects of BAE fieldwork that could not be measured with calipers, sketched, or weighed on a scale. Native language, for example, was recorded in lists of words and grammatical constructs, or in formulaic and often archaic set pieces such as mythic narrative, rather than in patterns of everyday speech. All linguistic fieldwork was conducted in this fashion at the time, but the use of the phonograph by government-sponsored ethnologists at the time yielded gratifyingly quantifiable evidence of productivity: shelves of cylinders faithfully enumerated for the benefit of Congress in each project report.

Practically speaking, the difficulties in tackling the ambitious task Powell set for the agency were immense within this acquisitive, item-centered, and museum-defined milieu. The BAE was never a large office, seldom exceeding the size of the first staff, which comprised six ethnologists, two philologists, a stenographer, and four clerks. Staff ethnologists engaged in some fieldwork, but most of the extensive collecting was accomplished by unsalaried individuals operating as consultants to the agency. All the early staff and consultants were self-educated in ethnology, coming from backgrounds as varied as zoology, music, and history of art (Judd 1967:11–13, 34). It was always a tumultuous swirl of competing temperaments, and the BAE was forever plagued by bureaucratic difficulties from without and within; Powell suffered his first stroke in the wake of a stormy session with staff consultant Matilda Coxe Stevenson, who was just as dictatorial with her supervisor as she was with her informants (Lurie 1966b:64). Under the circumstances, the achievement of the Bureau in amassing data in its eighty-five-year history is extraordinary.[11]

The BAE's professional staff for the most part lacked formal ethnographic, musicological, and linguistic training, and they labored under impossibly restrictive time constraints in the field. They found the introduction of the phonograph as a tool to be a godsend in the collection of the full textual material that, through Boas's influence, became a standard requirement in their work in the 1890s and early decades of the next century. W. H. Holmes, Powell's successor, described the advantages and limitation of the phonograph in a 1906 letter:

> I will say that the recording of phonetics of primitive languages by means of a phonograph of any construction is impossible, for the reason that the phonograph renders only the physical characteristics of the spoken sound, while the primary object we have to investigate is the physiological method of producing the sound. This can be obtained only by closest observation of the speaker.
>
> On the other hand, the phonograph is of very great value in recording the characteristic rhythm and cadence of the spoken languages and it also is of greatest service in obtaining native texts, undistorted by the difficulties of recording the spoken word in writing, which always necessitates slow pronunciation and for this reason breaks up the syntactic unity of the sentences. I have applied successfully the method of having old people, well versed in the lore of the Indians, tell their stories into the phonograph. Then I had the same stories in the presence of the original informant repeated by the phonograph to an interpreter, who pronounced the sentences as they appear on the phonograph to me, and

Figure 3.3. BAE ethnologist John Peabody Harrington at the Smithsonian, recording Cuna Indians Margarita Campos, Alfred Robinson, and James Perry. Courtesy of the Smithsonian Institution.

from this dictation I recorded the sentences, checking off the interpreter from the phonographic record. In these two respects the phonograph is the most useful instrument in linguistic studies. (Holmes 1906)

The device allowed them to record language, music, and ceremony—to "save the lore," in BAE ethnologist John Peabody Harrington's words—in a form from which they or others could later publish written phonetic and musical transcriptions, providing as well impressive quantifiable, artifactual evidence of their industry. Nearly a score of BAE consultants and staff made use of the phonograph from 1895 to the mid-1930s, creating an irreplaceable record of American Indian culture the value of which is still unfolding, as recordings of music and ceremony made during this era are recirculated among members of the communities in which they were originally recorded. This return of the recordings is not without irony, since both fieldworkers and often their subjects assumed that by the end of the twentieth century such communities would have long ceased to exist (Brady 1988:35–44).

The anthropological folklorists who reluctantly embraced the phonograph as an ethnographic tool viewed the texts they collected as a key to the understanding of larger issues in the groups they studied—as artifacts of evolutionary development, as evidence for migration and diffusion, or as templates revealing in microcosm the significant cultural patterns that played out in many aspects of social life. But there were also scholars who, by temperament or training, gravitated toward textual and musically expressive forms in their own right, without necessarily generalizing from them concerning broader cultural questions about the cultures from which the materials were collected (Zumwalt 1988:122). Musicologists and the scholars whom Rosemary Lévy Zumwalt labels "literary folklorists" both used the phonograph extensively in their work for reasons related to, but distinct from, the reasons motivating the anthropological collectors of folklore. No less an authority than Béla Bartók stated unequivocally, "The father of modern folksong studies was Thomas Edison" (1950:n.p.).

The earliest investigations concerning the purely musicological usefulness of the phonograph were undertaken by psychologist Benjamin Ives Gilman, to whom Mary Hemenway entrusted the analysis of the Zuni cylinders made by Fewkes in 1890. Gilman's work on these cylinders earned for him credit from pioneer ethnomusicologist Erich Moritz von Hornbostel as "the first scholar to use the phonograph in a scientific approach to the study of music" (Lee 1984a:vii). Gilman was primarily interested in the technical reliability of phonograph recordings and in their usefulness in comparative musicological studies. He scrupulously described his technique in transcribing the Fewkes cylinders. Using a harmonium tuned to concert pitch, he notated the programs of ten cylinders, having refrained from listening to any other Indian music so that his ear would be "clean." Despite the problems posed by fluctuations in the speed of recordings made with Fewkes's first machine, a treadle model, Gilman was enthusiastic about the accuracy of the phonograph:

> The apparatus proves to be a means by which the actual sound itself of which a music consists may, even in many of its more delicate characteristics, be stored up by the traveler, in a form permanently accessible to observation. . . . [the recording] can be interrupted at any point, repeated indefinitely, and even within certain limits magnified, as it were, for more accurate appreciation of changes in pitch, by increasing the duration of notes. A collection by phonographic cylinders like that obtained by Dr. Fewkes forms a permanent museum of primitive music, of which the specimens are comparable in fidelity of reproduction and convenience for study, to casts or photographs of sculpture or painting. (Gilman 1891:68)

Gilman's interest in the phonograph as a fieldwork tool was of the armchair variety: he was intrigued by the accuracy of the device because it suggested the possibility of a scientific study of comparative music. The machine raised "the hope that some proportion of the resulting close determinations of pitch might prove significant," revealing subtle "habitudes of performance" of different peoples and individuals (Gilman 1908:25). He grasped the distinction between the notation of a performance, which he believed only possible through the use of an objective mechanical device such as the phonograph, and the notation of a piece of music, the result of taking down by ear, which is "a record of the observer's idea of what the performers of certain observed sequences of tone would have performed had their execution corresponded to their intention, or (perhaps) had their intention not wandered also from a certain norm" (27). He concludes that notation made by ear from repeated hearings represents not observations but what he terms "a theory of observations"—the listener's paradigm for an ideal performance (25).

Gilman's work indirectly demonstrated an aspect of phonograph use unremarked upon at the time but significant nonetheless. He was essentially an indirect participant in the ethnographic process: Fewkes's cylinders offered a scholar far from Zuni a body of apparently objective data to work with—a separation virtually impossible under any other circumstance. Gilman's role in the early history of the phonograph is defined by this curious quality of separation from the source. His most important legacy aside from his work with Fewkes's Pueblo recordings is his 1893 anthology of 101 cylinders containing "exotic music" that he recorded at the World's Columbian Exposition in Chicago, which included Javanese, Samoan, Turkish, and Kwakiutl performances, a collection inspired and financed by the generous Mrs. Hemenway (Lee 1984a:viii).

Not all researchers were as impressed with the capacity of the phonograph to record musical performances. Musicologist H. E. Krehbiel, intrigued by Gilman's enthusiasm, pounced on the opportunity to test a machine on display at an exhibit in Frankfurt-on-Main. In a letter to the *Tribune* later printed in the *Musical Visitor*, he dismissed Gilman's assessment of the phonographic potential with an arch charm more deadly than any full-scale systematic critique: "I confess that I part with regret from the Zuni melodies which Dr. Fewkes imprisoned on his phonograph cylinder and Mr. Gilman transcribed for us (those quarter tones opened up such a delightful field for speculation); but since I toyed with a phonograph and pitch pipe at the Frankfurt exhibition yesterday they are banished from my collection" (Krehbiel 1891).

The dispute over the machine's usefulness in recording music remained unreconciled in Great Britain as well, but there the authoritative weight of opinion held against the phonograph. Like the American specialists in Indian linguistics, the British specialists in folksong placed great value on the skill required in making scrupulously accurate transcriptions—musical, in their case. It is perhaps no wonder, then, that Percy Grainger's vigorous recommendation of the phonograph as a tool met with such a cool reception on the part of the Folk-Song Society in 1908. In a letter commenting on a draft of Grainger's article "Collecting with the Phonograph" written for the Society journal, folksong doyenne Anne Geddes Gilchrist expressed her reservations to the equally eminent Lucy Broadwood:

> In my own experience of seeing records being taken by my brother of the performances of singers, both cultured and otherwise, we have found it not absolutely reliable as a recorder (though a good instrument). It is faulty both as regards "dynamics" and timbre of the sounds recorded, and fails to reproduce sibilants—the initial "s" of a word particularly. As to pitch, I have also had some occasional doubts as to which instrument—the human or the artificial—was a little "out"! The chief weakness of the phonograph, I think (apart from the general slight or more than slight distortion of tone) is its limited range of piano to forte. (Yates 1982:266)

For the trained musician, the fidelity of the phonograph clearly left something to be desired. The technical limitations led many collectors who used the machine to limit their performers to individuals whose vocal quality recorded well, and to restrict vocal mannerisms which would cause distortion (Hofmann 1968:101–13).

Paradoxically, despite technical reservations such as those quoted above, both Gilchrist and Cecil Sharp also objected to the phonograph as a means of recording that was *too* precisely accurate. They believed that ultimately the subjective response of the human ear best caught and conveyed the content of a performance. Although Sharp was to make use of the cylinder phonograph from time to time, he disliked the machine, expressing his reasons at some length in a letter to Percy Grainger in 1908. After remarking that he felt that it made singers self-conscious, that it was useless for singers whose voices were too weak to register, and that he was not satisfied with the clarity with which it recorded words, Sharp makes clear his most strenuous objection: that in the documentation of folksong "it is not an exact, scientifically accurate memorandum that is wanted, so much as a faithful artistic record of what is actually heard by the ordinary auditor." He comments that just as a photograph is generally inferior to a painting in conveying a scene, a phonographic recording is inferior to an auditor's rendering of a performance in standard notation (Yates

1982:269). This analogy was also drawn by Gilchrist, who passionately maintained that "the trained ear or eye of an artist is surely able to reproduce with more real *truth*—because with understanding and sympathy—the sounds or the sights impressing the sensitive surface—whether human or artificial—of an 'innocent' receptive medium" (Yates 1982:267).

Ideological objections also prevented the phonograph from becoming popular among many British collectors. To British folksong enthusiasts such as Gilchrist, Sharp, and Vaughan Williams, the introduction of a phonograph into the homes of their informants must have felt something like introducing a tightly leashed but hungry cat into a dovecote. Maud Karpeles relates: "More than once it happened that Cecil Sharp would be sitting quietly with an old couple, listening with enjoyment, when the peaceful atmosphere would be disturbed by the noisy entrance of the grandchildren, who would be shocked to find their grandparents singing their silly old songs to the gentleman, and would endeavor to reinstate the family reputation by turning on the gramophone with the latest music hall records; songs of which one old man said: 'Can't make no idea to it, no more than that chair; 'tis a gabble of noise with no meaning to it'" (1967:34).

The phonograph was the Enemy, the means of disseminating debased commercial products of the music hall among the as-yet "uncontaminated" rural populace. To use it in their work while attacking it in print must have struck them as inconsistent at the very least.[12] Of the powerful clique of musicians controlling the direction of the English Folk-Song Society, only Percy Grainger valued an initial recording of collected tunes in "as *merely scientific* a form as possible" (Yates 1982:266). Grainger's use of the adverb "merely" indicates his belief that the best transcriptions were those, technical or otherwise, that would give an objective rather than impressionistic rendering of a performance. In contrast, the interest of most members of the Society was aesthetically and, in a well-bred manner, sociologically motivated along a Romantic Herderian vein: to them, the subjectively modified response of an educated ear to a performance was intrinsic to the value of a transcription of folk music. Whereas the American collectors of American Indian material assumed that the technology represented by the phonograph would accelerate assimilation to Anglo society and thus improve the lot of the people they were recording, the British folksong collectors were for the most part musicians committed to the promulgation of folksong in an arranged and idealized form as the proper expression of the British people, to be preserved from the taint of progress.

American collectors of Anglo-American folksong were far readier to accept the advantages and make the best of the disadvantages of the phonograph than were their British counterparts. On the whole, the American folksong collectors of the cylinder era were not representatives of institutions or even participants in an organization with a fixed and clear program such as that of the English Folk-Song Society. They operated as private agents, fulfilling their own private agendas, often devoted to the folksong of a particular region. John A. Lomax, although supported by a Harvard traveling fellowship in his expeditions to collect cowboy songs in 1908–10, had no clear tie to the university aside from the sponsorship of George Lyman Kittredge and Barrett Wendell. Helen Harkness Flanders devoted herself wholeheartedly to Vermont folksong, independent of any institutional agenda or program. Phillips Barry similarly devoted himself to New England in general. To these private scholars and local enthusiasts the phonograph was a boon precisely because they were *not* accomplished, professionally skilled musicians. It allowed them to collect extensively without the proficiency demanded by transcription by hand. Folksong scholars in the tradition of Francis James Child and George Lyman Kittredge, their primary interest was in the texts of the songs, but they were too thorough to neglect melody when a simple means of collecting it was available.

The machine was also valued by small regional societies, groups of amateur scholars devoted to the lore of their area, who worried that the material they sought to collect would be gone forever before they could set it down. Alice Mabel Bacon, reporting on the work and methods of the Hampton Folk-Lore Society of Virginia in 1898, lamented the delay in collecting African-American music in her region, giving as a reason the lack of any professional musician in the club to transcribe. "If we can obtain a graphophone, and thus make records not only of songs, but of sermons, prayers, etc., and so gather, as we cannot now gather, some complete records of entire religious services, we are convinced that through this means we may add much to the common fund of knowledge of the Negro music" (Bacon 1898:19–20).

The urgency expressed by the Hampton Folk-Lore Society is typical of the sentiments of the local enthusiasts as well as those scholars engaged in the collection of Indian cultural expression. For individuals convinced that each passing day diminished the harvest of traditional materials to be gathered, the phonograph, whatever its limitations, offered exceptional speed and efficiency in the field.

The efficiency of the phonograph as a tool in the field was reiterated by Marius Barbeau in a programmatic address to the American Folklore Society in 1918, a plea for consistent professional standards in the documentation of fieldwork. An experienced collector equipped with a phonograph, he said, could make an adequate record of data in a single day that an untrained observer will only imperfectly record in a month of work; with good informants, an expert field folklorist "finds no difficulty in collecting an average of forty or fifty songs or ballads in a day's work, the texts being taken in stenography, and a few stanzas recorded on the phonograph" (Barbeau 1919:195). The collector today trembles not only at the demands such an "average" day's work would represent, even with a tape recorder, but also at the staggering richness of available materials the offhand reference to forty or fifty song texts implies!

Despite its many limitations, the phonograph represented a valued tool for many collectors in the early part of the century; it could expedite fieldwork undertaken under pressure, produce a body of data conforming to contemporary notions of scientific objectivity, and compensate for skills many collectors lacked in written transcription of music of phonetic texts. In addition, for many women collectors, it may have represented compensation of another order.

The typical role of women in the late nineteenth and early twentieth centuries located her at the protected center of the domestic nest—a role turned topsy-turvy in virtually every significant respect by the requirements of serious and extended field research. Indeed, this very inversion of gender expectations may account for the surprisingly large number of women who made substantive contributions in the area—women whose professional activities in anthropology and folklore included a social agenda, overt or covert. Whether or not they framed their involvement in fieldwork as revolutionary—and some did—the adventure of escaping the usual routine of women's lives of the period was intensely attractive to a wide range of temperaments, from indomitable Matilda Coxe Stevenson to gentle Helen Heffron Roberts.

Escape into a male-dominated professional sphere had its price. Franz Boas was exceptional in his encouragement of women as ethnographers, but his sponsorship was not an entree into the almost exclusively male precinct of institutional employment (Deacon 1997:258–72). Relatively few women had had access to even the limited formal academic training available in fieldwork-related disciplines at the turn of the century, and they were further burdened with the expectation that their work would display an inappropriate level of "feminine" subjectivity. Perhaps reacting to these critical stereotypes, a striking number of women collectors used the phonograph expertly and extensively, including Alice Cunningham Fletcher, Elsie Clews Parsons, Constance Goddard DuBois, Helen Heffron Roberts, Laura Boulton, Natalie Curtis Burlin, Helen Hartness Flanders, Gladys Reichard, Theodora Kroeber, and the tireless Frances Densmore.

Not only was the phonograph a useful tool in preempting sexist assumptions concerning the nature of the data collected by women but mastery of its technology also implied a satisfyingly "masculine" proficiency in mechanical matters usually considered a male preserve. Such symbolic appropriation of "manly" skill in emergent technologies was a notable feature of gender politics of the period—Jane Gay, Alice Cunningham Fletcher's companion in the field, wrote lively popular accounts of their adventures among the Nez Perce in which she habitually referred to herself in the third person as "she" when her role was that of "the Cook," but "*he*" when acting as "the Photographer" (Mark 1988:185). The use of up-to-date equipment provided an emblem of competence for women in the field, allowing them to demonstrate facility in areas usually marked off as male territory.[13]

In the end, both men and women accepted or rejected the phonograph for a variety of reasons. For some, it provided a convenient and practical means to document the forms of verbal and musical expression considered the essential units of a community's traditional culture; others considered it too cumbersome and intrusive to use on a regular basis. Some collectors welcomed the opportunity to make use of a dynamic new technological innovation; others saw the very novelty of the phonograph, and the social change its dissemination heralded, as a symptom of precisely that progressive force against which they were valiantly holding the line. Some regarded the device as a means to achieve a scientific objectivity in their work; others saw it as a cheap evasion of the skill in transcription essential to any well-trained ethnographer.

Then as now, every fieldworker engages not only in a professional process of documentation and analysis but also in an inner enactment of a privately composed drama as suspenseful, risky, and exhilarating as the hunt—a heroic drama in which we cast ourselves as protagonist. In the end, the choice each fieldworker made concerning the use of the phonograph often depended on a combination of practical and ideological factors—but depended as well on how readily he or she accepted the role of the phonograph as a dramatis persona in the fieldwork scenario. A clumsy prop? A steady supporting performer? Or even an upstaging scene-stealer? The phonograph could be any of these.

But the performers had strong feelings about the process, and their reaction to the use of the phonograph in recording their lore indicates that they cast both the device and its operators in unexpected parts in their own mise-en-scène—as will be seen in the next chapter.

Performers and the Phonograph

The Box That Got the Flourishes

> A dance had been announced for a certain night, and I made an early appearance on the ground. While I was waiting for the festivities to start, a young man named Wolf-lies-down (as I found out later) accosted me amiably in fair English and was curious about my business. Was I trying to buy horses on the reservation? I bethought myself of what I had once read in Herbert Spencer's essays on education, to whit, that in teaching a child one should always proceed from the concrete to the abstract; and what held for children would surely be appropriate for aborigines. So I answered somewhat as follows: "Well, I am here to talk with your old men to find out how they used to hunt and play and dance. I want to hear them tell stories of ancient times. . . ." But at this point young Wolf-lies-down, who had never been off the reservation, interrupted me with, "Oh, I see, you are an ethnologist."
>
> *Robert H. Lowie (1959:60)*

One of the lesser known fables of Aesop recounts a meeting between a man and a lion before a vast mural realistically depicting a triumphant hunter, his foot on the neck of the vanquished king of beasts. Concerned about his companion's reaction to the piece, the man turns inquiringly to the lion, who merely curls his lip and shrugs, "So, who painted the lion?" Written from the point of view of the collectors, most accounts of fieldwork activity in which ethnographers appear at all tend to depict them triumphant—resourceful, adroit, accepted, even beloved. Reading these accounts, members of the communities in question might suggest, like the lion, that the scene could be repainted from another point of view. Few ethnographers have shared Robert Lowie's willingness to depict himself in as unflattering a light as in his revealing encounter with Wolf-lies-down.

Implicit in most early ethnographic collections are three assumptions concerning interactions in the field: the collector is in control of the event, the full cooperation of the performer is achieved without reflection or negotiation, and unsatisfactory recordings are owing to shortcomings on the part of the performer, or, when the phonograph was used, nervousness over the mechanical process of recording or malfunction of the device. The phonograph itself represented a kind of emblem of authority for the collector; as its operator, he or she felt securely in control of the episode. Frances Densmore's 1940 instructions to a neophyte collector exude a quelling impression of the lengths to which some collectors would go to achieve a technically accomplished recording:

> The psychology of managing the Indians so as to secure the best songs, sung in the desired manner, is the most important factor in the work, in my opinion. I will take pleasure in giving you the benefit of my experience in this regard. I had to formulate my own method, but I find it gives equally good results in all tribes. . . .
>
> Before actual recording is begun, it is sometimes a good plan to have an "open house" where everyone is shown the apparatus, sees it in use, and, perhaps, some test records may be made at this time—so all curiosity is satisfied. This may be followed by a promise that everyone can come again, and hear the records, if they will keep away while the work is in progress.
>
> Only the interpreter and singer should be present when the songs are recorded unless they want a "witness" or someone to consult.
>
> Only one singer at a time, unless the records are for "exhibition purposes," and to show concerted singing.
>
> An Indian drum does not record well, and a rattle does not record at all. A short stick on a pasteboard box gives the percussion without resonance, which is all that is wanted unless the records are for exhibition use. . . .
>
> Each song should be sung through several times, followed by a distinct pause. Singers should not be allowed to *run their songs together.*
>
> It is safest to get information before recording the song. Translations can safely follow the recording.

All yells must be strictly forbidden, if the records are to be transcribed. It is also a waste of space on the blank to let them "talk," and announce the song in the native language, etc.

It does not pay to have them "rehearse" a song audibly—they should "run it over in their mind," then record it. Often, a "rehearsal," which is not recorded, is better than the recording.

The singer must never be allowed to think that he is in charge of the work. A strict hold must be kept on him.

Singers should be checked by general reputation. Loud voices are not essential, and men who sing at dances are apt to be too free-and-easy.

It is not wise to take too many songs from one singer, nor let a man sing too long at a time. (Gray 1988:ix)

Not all collectors using the phonograph were as rigid or systematic as Frances Densmore, but all had to evolve negotiating strategies to achieve cooperation from their singers, and all had to accommodate the technical limitations of the machine by adjustment of performers to an unnatural performance context.

Despite the apparent control of the encounter exerted by the collector as operator of the machine, the process of negotiation involved in its use may actually have altered the power dynamics in favor of the performer. Robert A. Georges and Michael Owen Jones have observed that, because fields for folklore and anthropology require fieldwork as a professional activity, folklorists and anthropologists are singularly vulnerable to their informants (1980). Fieldworkers depicted themselves in control of the collecting process, in Densmore's words, "managing the Indians so as to secure the best songs," but in practice the mechanical nature of the phonograph required a much higher degree of compliance, even collaboration, than documentation consisting of simple observation and note taking—a process in which the question might well be raised concerning who was in fact being managed. The performer and collector had to agree on a time and place to record—documenting social or ritual events in situ was out of the question. The performer had to show up—no small matter in cultures in which the concept of "an appointment" was non-existent. Selections that would record effectively had to be agreed upon. And

Figure 4.1. Frances Densmore and Blackfoot singer Mountain Chief.
Courtesy of the Smithsonian Institution.

finally, in the process of recording itself, once the needle engaged the wax, the performer and the phonograph formed a dyad as intimate as that of two dancers; the attention and voice poured directly into the horn of the machine, effectively excluding the collector for the duration of the piece.

As she herself reported, Densmore was at least once outmaneuvered in a strategic duel centering on the use of the phonograph. When working among the Uinta and White River bands of Northern Utes at Fort Duquesne, Utah, in 1914, she found little initial cooperation. The Utes were unmoved by the offer of payment and the promise of preservation of the recordings, and made her work the object of open ridicule. Uneasily she insisted on a formal meeting with their chief, Red Cap, despite the fact that she had seen him and noted that "his face wore the smile I do not like to see on the face of an Indian." She prepared her borrowed office carefully, placing an American flag over the chair for the Chief. When he arrived, she addressed him with consciously assumed dignity, reminding him of her adoption by the Sioux chief Red Fox and warning that she would tell her Indian father of her rude treatment at the hands of the Utes.

Red Cap listened attentively through his interpreter, then informed her that he would ensure the cooperation of his best singer. He even remained for the duration of an entirely satisfactory session. But Red Cap had a countermove to play:

> After the recording was finished, Red Cap said, "I have done as you wished. Now I want to ask a favor. I do not sing, as I said, but I would like to talk into your phonograph. Will it record talking?" Guilelessly I said it would record any song.
>
> "Well," said the wily old chief, "Then I will talk and I want you to play the record for the Indian Commissioner in Washington. I want to tell him that we do not like this Agent. We want him sent someplace else. We don't like the things he does. What we tell him does not get to the Commissioner but I want the Commissioner to hear my voice. I want you to play this so he will hear my words, and I want you to give him a good translation of my speech. We want to get rid of this agent." (Densmore [1917a] 1968:39–43)

Densmore had received a favor from Red Cap and was obliged to agree to his request. Six months later she kept her promise to the chief—in part. She played the recording of his speech to Cato Sells, Commissioner of Indian Affairs. Alas for Red Cap's diplomacy: after an explanation from Densmore, the speech was played without comment or translation. Densmore concludes, "Numerous employees of the Indian Office were asked to hear the recordings, but no one understood the Ute language and the contents of the speech remained a mystery. The record has not been played since that day."[1] Despite the failed outcome of Red Cap's ploy, he controlled the encounter with Densmore masterfully, placing her in his debt before advancing his request and making canny use of the cylinder phonograph as a political tool.

The relationship between fieldworker and informant during the era of the cylinder phonograph must be reexamined in all its intricacy in order to evaluate the effect of the machine on the interaction. As Lowie demonstrates in the anecdote quoted above, many fieldworkers infantilized their subjects to an extent that not only insulted their hosts but disgusted white observers as well.[2] Objectionable in itself, this practice also placed the collectors at a disadvantage in evaluating the complex motives that led to cooperation in the documentation of native culture, effectively blinding them to the extent to which their performers were active collaborators in the ethnographic process.

Many fieldworkers seem to have been relatively unaware of their informants' personal reactions to the mission of the newcomer in the community and the process of collecting cultural data; if such a sensitivity on the part of the collector existed it was not usually expressed in published form. Alice C. Fletcher's success has been attributed to gratitude for her private generosity and courtesy toward the Omaha and Osage as well as her vigorous legislative activity on their behalf—an irony, since it appears that the latter, well-intentioned though it was, had a disastrous effect on those she was trying to assist, as she herself became aware even at the time (Judd 1967:53; Lurie 1966a:31–33, 80–85; Mark 1988:169–79). More aggressive individuals are portrayed as succeeding by sheer force of character: Matilda Coxe Stevenson, one of the original staff consultants of the Bureau of American Ethnology, was celebrated in popular newspapers for having subdued a threatening "savage" by beating him about the head with her umbrella, and reportedly knew no scruples in her endeavors to document Zuni religious ceremonies, taking surreptitious photographs and possibly even stealing sacred objects. John P. Harrington's determination to "give not the yawning grave its plunder" and "save, save the lore for future ages' joy" resulted in a relentless fieldwork style, which inspired the jibe among BAE colleagues that he had "worried more `last survivors' to death than any other of his profession" (Judd 1967:46).

Frances Densmore wrote that when a collecting trip among the Utes lasted longer than she had estimated for them, she was directly challenged by a member of the group: "Why aren't you gone? You said that you would go at a certain time and you are still here. We don't like it. How much longer are you going to stay and what are you doing here, anyway?" (Densmore [1917a] 1968:43). Emotions concerning collectors seem to have run particularly high in Southwestern Indian communities such as the Hopi and Zuni, partly because these groups have been the object of such intense ethnological interest and partly because the highly secret and sacred nature of their ceremonial life has stimulated some collectors to boorish and intrusive tactics. Indian anthropologist Alphonso Ortiz recalls: "I never considered majoring in anthropology as an undergraduate because I met too many members of the field who regarded it as a sacred calling and operated as if they had an inherent and inalienable right to the information they were seeking; the Pueblos seemed to attract them because of the challenge. Their rule is 'anything goes,' and the system of morality they bring to their dealings with Indians is akin to that of the heroin pusher." Ortiz remarks that anthropologists, who are, after all, relatively benign in comparison to some other intruders into Indian life, are often singled out for abuse: "The characteristics that anthropologists seem to have uniquely are a high degree of visibility and vulnerability. There is not much a lone Indian can do about the BIA, but he can certainly kick the hell out of the resident anthropologist" (1971:12–13).

Ortiz's comments are gentle in comparison to those of Vine Deloria, who does not even allow the anthropologist the useful if ignominious function of a scapegoat. An entire chapter of *Custer Died for Your Sins* is devoted to the flagellation of the profession. Anthropologists are accused of being both ineffectual and egregiously destructive to the social and economic welfare of the people they study. "Into each life, it is said, some rain must fall. Some people have bad horoscopes, others take tips on the stock market. . . . But Indians are cursed above all other people in history. Indians have anthropologists" (1969:40). Though the tone is flip, the message is serious; given a choice between repelling cavalry attacks and the descent of the anthropologists, Deloria proposes attending first to the latter: "In a crisis situation men always attack the biggest threat to their existence" (Deloria 1969:78).

This latter-day savaging of collectors is not limited to American Indian spokesmen. The Irish writer Flann O'Brien extended the comprehensive embrace of his misanthropy to include folklorists in his brilliant Gaelic novel *The Poor Mouth*. In the fictional region of Corkadoragha a poor family resorts to clothing their pigs in trousers in order to trick a nearsighted government inspector deputed to pay two pounds a head to those parents raising their children to speak English instead of Irish. Meanwhile, a folklorist from Dublin has arrived: "He had an instrument called a gramophone and this instrument was capable of memorizing all it heard if anyone narrated stories or old lore to it; it could also spew out all it heard whenever one desired it. It was a wonderful instrument and frightened many people in the area and struck others dumb; it is doubtful whether its like will ever be here again. Since folks thought that it was unlucky, the gentleman had a difficult time collecting the folklore tales from them" (1974:42–45). The collector resorts to whiskey to unlock their tongues, but only succeeds in strewing the pub with inarticulate and sodden bodies. Suddenly a stranger pushes open the unlatched door, creeping into the room in a thoroughly intoxicated fashion but muttering Gaelic of the highest order. "It appeared that the gentleman thought Gaelic was extremely difficult and he was overjoyed that the machine was absorbing it; he understood that good Gaelic is difficult but the best Gaelic is well-nigh unintelligible" (44). The gentleman makes his scholarly reputation on these recordings, taking them to Berlin where he receives an honorary degree for a collection "so good, so poetic, so obscure [that] there was no fear for Gaelic the while the like was audible in Ireland" (45). The bemused narrator concludes that he himself is not certain whether the language recorded was English, Gaelic, or dialect, but one thing is certain: the recordings were taken from one of his family's wandering trousered pigs. Flann O'Brien, born prior to the establishment of the Irish Republic and its official encouragement of Gaelic, was bitterly aware of the irony by which an outsider culture schemed to discourage the speaking of Gaelic on one hand, and on the other rewarded those who "preserved" it mechanically as an academic curiosity.

The lack of sources other than writings of the collectors themselves makes it virtually impossible to determine the extent to which the anger in these characterizations of O'Brien, Ortiz, and Deloria may have been prevalent in communities visited by anthropologists and folklorists during the era of the cylinder phonograph or whether they are the product of an accumulation of bitterness over what is derided by natives as a century of ethnological flimflam. Anthropologist Keith Basso estimates that the formularized joking routines he describes parodying "the Whiteman" are a fairly recent phenomenon among the Western Apache, dating back no more than forty years—the period in which interaction with Anglo-Americans was becoming a daily occurrence (1979:29). Yet as early as 1894, the ethnologist Francis La Flesche, Omaha himself, revealed his ambivalence concerning study of his people in a letter to the Reverend J. Owen Dorsey: "Too much of the private affairs of many of the Omaha have been published [by the BAE] without their consent, and I do not wish to add more" (Judd 1967:52).

Interestingly, in all these accounts of hostility there is no indication that the anger was displaced from the collector to his or her phonograph. Given the discomfort that collectors expected to find in their informants with regard to the machine, one might anticipate instances of the cylinders being destroyed or phonographic equipment being stolen. No such incidents were reported. Rather, the expressions of hostility are directed explicitly and appropriately toward the fieldworkers themselves, not their mechanical tools.

Even when the collector created a negative impression, social, economic, or political pressures within the traditional life of a community could result in cooperation on the part of performers. Social pressures inhering in the traditional ways of a community could result in serious dilemmas for the potential informant. In some cultures a tradition of unstinting courtesy and hospitality allowed the collector, intentionally or unintentionally, to impose upon hosts' time and resources. Among the joking routines described by Basso are a number based on a portrait of the importunate and disingenuous "Whiteman" who is ever ready to manipulate an Apache out of valued possessions by the device of admiring them inordinately, manipulating social norms to achieve selfish ends (Basso 1979:86–87). Vine Deloria relates a story, which he feels represents the exaggerated patience and courtesy general to all Indians, concerning a Cherokee who lost his wife, children, cattle, and farm to a white man. The Indian pursued him for years, and finally caught up with him. " 'Are you the guy who did all these things,' the Cherokee asked. Yes, the man admitted, he was the one. 'Well, you better watch that crap,' the Cherokee warned." Deloria goes on to express his fear that "we will be so damn polite that we will lose everything for fear of hurting someone's feelings if we object to the way things are going" (1969:277). In many instances the collectors may have been naive, even unscrupulous, in their assessment of the burden placed on informants by their cooperation with research.

As mere individuals the collectors could not hope to offer much in return for cooperation aside from gratitude and friendship—the latter of a temporary order, because they seldom lived in proximity to the communities from which they sought information. They could, however, make the choice to cooperate more alluring by offering payment for cooperation. This remuneration usually took the form of cash or liquor, carrying with it the danger that the need for such payment would result in compromised material. Although it was illegal to sell alcohol to reservation Indians, little could be done to prevent the gift of a bottle (Lurie 1966b:64). Straightforward cash payment for assistance was also common: at one time, Frances Densmore's rate was a quarter a song, although other collectors chose to pay for a block of time rather than item by item (1917a:40). Matilda C. Stevenson created a stir among accountants who reviewed her BAE expense account and found the cryptic entry "One man, one night, one dollar" in her request for reimbursement (Lurie 1966b:64).[3]

In the case of those individuals whose participation involved considerable time, payment was ideally about commensurate with the value of the work time lost, although this was by no means always the understanding on both sides. The blues singer Son House recalled a full day spent in making disc recordings for Alan Lomax in the early 1940s, at a time when the musician had already made a professional name, only to find that the extent of his payment was to be free Coca-Cola—though, as he ruefully remembered, the Coke was good and cold (Charters 1967:66).

The Lomaxes, on their shoestring budget operating out of the Library of Congress, and the BAE collectors, who followed a different policy of remuneration, both had in common another important incentive for cooperation, the strength of which they themselves sometimes failed to comprehend fully: they were based in Washington, D.C. For North American informants, Indian or otherwise, the nation's capital then as now evoked an image of power. John A. Lomax for a time had all his singers recite a set formula at the beginning of each recording to the effect that they were giving the performance to the American people to be kept for posterity at the Library of Congress in Washington, D.C.—a statement that effectively assured them of the importance of their contribution, reminding them of the authority behind Lomax's mission, and serving as a kind of rudimentary release agreement with regard to payment and subsequent use of the material. In the course of her work for the BAE, Frances Densmore told singers that their voices would be stored on the cylinders in Washington in a building that would never burn down. She can be heard on one cylinder recording encouraging a Lac Du Flambeau singer by telling him that his voice was so fine she would send it all the way to Washington (Hofmann 1968:24; Brady 1984:22).

Among native informants the potency represented by an official Washington connection could have an almost mythic dimension far out of proportion to any concrete favors anticipated from the contact. In *Diplomats in Buckskins*, a history of Indian delegations in Washington, Herman J. Viola describes the high regard Indians still hold for the city of Washington, quoting Henry Old Coyote of the Crow tribe who served as a Senate advisor on Indian legislation in 1978: "Indians love their country and this country is administered by the government so they tie the two of them together. They show respect to the government." For Old Coyote and his people, Washington represents that government. "It's the nation's capital, that's where the president resides. It's more like a shrine to Indians . . . and they hold it as such and they feel that reverence should be extended to the place" (1981:55). Trips to Washington by tribal representatives still form an important part of Indian diplomacy; in the early years of the century some of these trips incidentally provided opportunities for phonographic sessions at the BAE offices at the Smithsonian and other locations in Washington (Brady 1984:47, 93).

Some collectors did engage in shaping official policy regarding Indians, but the results were seldom fortunate. Alice C. Fletcher's participation in the drafting of land allotment legislation to the Omaha, Winnebago, and Nez Perce unintentionally led to economic and social disaster for the tribes concerned (Lurie 1966a). Neither the Library of Congress nor the Bureau of American Ethnology ever had a direct or significant effect on public policy concerning the peoples visited by their collectors, but this fact was not always recognized by informants hoping for influence in Washington. Not only did they hope to create a good impression on visitors from the seat of power, potential performers were also influenced by the idea that records of their traditions were valued enough to be stored in a federal agency in the capital city where they could "speak for" the people recorded.

Collectors need not have been official representatives of a Washington institution to bring considerable official pressure to bear on potential performers. Although Alice Fletcher's first journey to Omaha, Nebraska, in 1881 was a private research trip, she bristled with official support, bearing letters from the Secretary of War, the Secretary of the Interior, the Postmaster General, and an impressive array of college professors. As it happens she found this ammunition more useful in subduing savage agents, with whom her relations were frequently strained, than in securing cooperation of the Omaha (Lurie 1966a:33; Mark 1988:64–79).

Other collectors, however, made it a point to maintain close diplomatic relations with Bureau of Indian Affairs agents, missionaries, state officials, and other representatives of Anglo temporal and spiritual authority, depending on their hospitality and guidance in pursuing fieldwork investigations. This was necessary and understandable given the brevity of most field trips of the period, but it had a problematic effect on the materials gathered. The individuals recommended by local authorities as competent assistants, translators, and informants were those whose cooperation could be assured by the authority—that is, they had already established themselves as reliably competent in or comfortable with Anglo-American culture and were in some instances regarded as marginal or suspect by other members of the community.

In her sessions with the phonograph, Frances Densmore specifically sought translators to assist her who had been educated in the use of "literary" English idiom, preferably those who had been trained at Hampton Normal and Industrial Institute, Carlisle School, or other similar institutions of higher learning (Densmore [1917b] 1968:104; see also Lowie 1959:12). Alice Fletcher relied on the Omaha family of Joseph La Flesche, himself the son of a French trader and an Omaha mother. Joseph La Flesche had insisted on a Presbyterian mission education for his son Francis despite the boy's desire to remain at home. His daughter Bright Eyes (Susette) La Flesche had conducted a brilliantly successful tour of the East in the 1870s, lecturing on Indian rights. It was from the La Flesche family that Alice Fletcher derived both her initial entree to the tribe and the foundation of her ideas concerning the best interests of the tribe politically and economically. The La Flesche family members were influential but by no means typical of their people: the site of the La Flesche home near Macy, Nebraska, is still known to some local Omaha as the Village of the Make-Believe Whitemen (Lurie 1966a). The tendency to rely on highly acculturated assistants and informants was natural and probably necessary for most collectors, but such a pattern does raise certain questions concerning the typical nature of the material collected through their efforts. This was especially true in instances such as Densmore's expeditions where the cylinder phonograph streamlined the operation to such an extent that little actual time was spent living in or becoming familiar with the community.

The local authorities who directed the collector to assistants of suitable background could guarantee a forced cooperation from certain individuals. John Whiting was accompanied by an Australian government patrol officer when he arrived to do fieldwork among the Kwoma in the 1930s. The officer ordered the villagers to build Whiting a house and threatened punishment to anyone who proved troublesome to him, thus automatically labeling him as "government protected" (Paul 1953:433–34). Densmore was assisted in Fort Yates, North Dakota, by a prisoner from the guardhouse "lent" to her by the superintendent (Densmore [1917b] 1968:105). Prisoners represented a virtual stock-in-trade of the field trips undertaken by John and Alan Lomax in 1933 and 1934: they were besieged with pleas for intercession and did in fact arrange commutation of the sentence of Iron Head Baker (Porterfield 1996:375).[4]

The performances of the prisoners may for the most part have been willing, but they were not necessarily voluntary. John A. Lomax writes of one instance in which a prisoner whom the warden knew to be a good blues singer was called upon to sing on a Sunday. He objected to singing worldly music, especially on the Lord's Day, but the warden insisted. When the machine began to roll, the prisoner surprised all by prefacing his song with an apology to God, expressing faith that He would understand that this song was not going to be sung by choice (Lomax 1947:150–51). Far from being abashed by the episode, Lomax enjoyed recounting it.

Internal and external social pressures such as those discussed above as well as a naturally uneasy response to a stranger and a strange situation gave rise to certain responses unanticipated and poorly understood by most collectors. The collector often became the butt of jokes that depended on an insider's knowledge of the informant's culture and language. Humorous nicknames offered a spurious badge of acceptance while playing on the collector's linguistic ignorance: Franz Boas was referred to by some Kwakiutl as "the Fart," and Matilda Coxe Stevenson boasted of a Pueblo name she was told meant "Little Flower" or "Little Mother" but which in fact meant "She with Big Broad Buttocks Like a Mesa" (Guillemin 1975:300–301). Robert H. Lowie turned his role as the object of amusement to his advantage by consciously playing along; in learning the Crow language his attempts to master various tongue-twisters and rhymes tickled his audience, and he never failed to crack them up completely with his feeling delivery of the line "All the whites are bad, I alone am good" (Lowie 1959:57–58). By allowing himself to appear ridiculous, Lowie sacrificed his image of himself as competent and in charge, but what he lost in dignity he probably regained in the enhancement of his relationship with the Crow people.

The cylinder phonograph offered informants an excellent opportunity to vent their feelings concerning the collector in humor. The Hopi clowning imitation of a collector with a phonograph in the course of the Basket Dance celebration in the late 1890s, described in chapter 2, indicates the comic potential that informants recognized in the fieldwork sessions, particularly with regard to the seriousness with which the collectors treated their machines. Fewkes reported that the Zuni silversmith Kuishte on first seeing the phonograph demonstrated said to him in Spanish, "Melicano [the American] sabe mucho"; this may have been a serious response, but it is possible also to read in it an ironical comment on the self-importance of the "Melicano" (Fewkes 1890a:1095).

Manifestations such as these undoubtedly represent only a small proportion of joking behavior at the expense of the collector and his machine, as they are the mocking expressions actually observed, though not necessarily understood, by the objects of their humor. It is likely that mannerisms perceived as characteristically Anglo-American, such as restless preoccupation with mechanical devices, impertinent interrogation in conversation, unnecessary statements concerning feelings and responses, and self-promotion as the Indians' friend and advocate, may have resulted in various formularized private routines based on the inappropriate behavior of "the Whiteman" similar to those described in detail by Keith H. Basso among contemporary Western Apache (Basso 1979:37–64).

The tension in most communities introduced by ethnological investigations is not necessarily a simple product of the ambiguity of a fieldworker's anomalous position in the group or the social uneasiness that inevitably accompanies encounters on cultural frontiers. During the era of the cylinder phonograph the consequences risked in cooperating with fieldworkers could be considerably more serious than offended feelings and disrupted routines, particularly in American Indian communities. Fieldworkers, especially those using the phonograph, were in search of the most ancient expressions of song and narrative; the more secret and sacred the material, the more desirable it became in the eyes of the researcher.

Penetrating the religious mysteries of other cultures added to the prestige of the investigator in his own realm. Frank Cushing fulfilled the ambition of many a fieldworker when he was made a Zuni Bow priest in the course of his work in the 1880s; subsequently the deaths of three high priests of the community were attributed to their participation in his induction (Pandey 1972:323). The Hunkpapa Sioux priests who revealed the secret White Buffalo ceremony to Alice C. Fletcher in the 1880s agonized over the danger such a breach of taboo posed to the community, which blamed several near-disasters on her presence and activities. One of the priests entreated her, "Promise me by your God that no harm shall come to me or to my people because I have spoken to you of these sacred things" (Mark 1988:83). The venerable Omaha singer Xutha Watonin, who died shortly after recording with Francis La Flesche in 1916, was said to have been killed in retribution for having divulged sacred material (Bureau of American Ethnology 1917:59–60; La Flesche 1927–1928:533–38). Although less well substantiated in the reports of the time, the rumor remains current today among the Omaha that La Flesche's informant Saucy Calf was murdered in 1912 for his recording of sacred material; this story was related to a staff member of the Federal Cylinder Project in the course of discussions concerning dissemination of material collected from the Omaha and Osage tribes. The use of the cylinder phonograph could increase the element of risk in sharing such material: the recorded cylinder was irrefutable evidence that such illicit cooperation had taken place.[5] A collector who failed to return with good material might lose his or her reputation or job, but an informant who imprudently participated in a fieldwork session might lose more than livelihood.

Fear of supernatural reprisal could also prevent an otherwise willing subject from performing. Constance Goddard DuBois lost the opportunity to record valuable material from a Luiseno singer in 1906: "One of my storytellers was about to sing with great reluctance some songs descended to him from his father, when an apparition of Chaup or Takwish, the electrical fire-ball or meteor, in broad daylight, so terrified him as an omen that he refused to reveal anything further" (1908:76n6). We have already encountered Sukmit of Pit River, who believed that the phonograph would be too much for his spiritual assistant (de Angelo 1973:63).

Edmund Nequatewa relates a chilling story still current among the Hopi of Walpi concerning Jesse Walter Fewkes that accounts for his abrupt departure from the Pueblo in the fall of 1898. Although the annual report of the director of the BAE gave an outbreak of smallpox as the reason for Fewkes's leave-taking, according to Nequatewa the ethnologist told the priests of the kiva that he had received a mysterious supernatural visitation. In the course of the Wuwuchim ceremonies Fewkes was dismissed from the kiva for the celebration of the holiest part of the ritual. He returned to his house and began to write up his notes. Suddenly he was joined by Masauwu, the earth god, who terrorized Fewkes with his horrible aspect and frightening behavior until he agreed to adopt Hopi ways and believe in Masauwu, with the implied injunction that he would discontinue his inquiry. Once Fewkes acceded to these demands, the being cast a spell on him and they played like little children for the rest of the night. Fewkes left the Pueblo shortly thereafter (Nequatewa 1980:36–37). The story suggests a terrible supernatural risk associated with inappropriate inquiry into religious matters—a risk incurred by singers as well as collectors. Performers who chose to share such sacred knowledge must have had compelling motives for doing so; there must have been more than a simple, passive accedence to the will of a stranger with a machine.

In instances where collectors were aware of tension in their relationships with informants, collectors were often inclined to blame the phonograph as the villain of the scenario, fearing solicitously that the machine would make the performers self-conscious or fearful. Characteristic of these expressions of concern are the remarks of Helen H. Roberts, quoted in chapter 3, in which she regrets the loss, in using the phonograph, of a more human informality and flexibility built into the process of transcription by hand. This concern extended beyond fieldwork in tribal communities: Cecil Sharp, too, disliked the phonograph because he felt it was impossible when using it to get a relaxed, natural performance from a singer. Taking issue with Percy Grainger's advocacy of the phonograph as a tool in the field, Sharp wrote to him in a letter dated 1908:

> In my own somewhat limited experience I have found singers, although not at all unwilling to sing into the phonograph, yet quite incapable of singing into it in their usual un-selfconscious manner. I remember spending an hour or more last Christmas holiday with a singer (from whom I have, in the course of the last few years, taken down a very large number of songs) in the vain attempt to secure an accurate phonograph record of his singing of "Lady Maisry." He was a young man, a very first-rate folk-singer, and not by any means a nervous subject. His first attempt failed dismally; he forgot his words, pitched his song too high, sang much faster than usual, and altogether fell far below his usual standard of performance. I then stopped the phonograph and made him sing through the song in the ordinary manner. This he at once did in his accustomed way, without hesitancy, or mistake. Then I put him at the phonograph again, with precisely the same disastrous result as before. I repeated the experiment yet once more, but with no better fortune. Finally I gave up the attempt as hopeless. (Yates 1982:268)

Grainger, on the other hand, felt that the singers' excitement over the process of mechanical recording actually improved performances collected with the phonograph (1909:147).

In recent years much—though some still would say not enough—has been written concerning the cross-cultural tensions aroused by anthropological fieldwork and the dangers posed to the ethnographer's work and person.[6] This is all to the good: collectors cannot be too sensitive to the fact that their presence affects the community; scholars cannot be too aware that the ethnographic works on which they base their writings were not collected in a social vacuum but by people from people. But so obvious as to have received scant notice, the fact remains that an immense quantity of ethnographic material has been collected, and by no means all of it from reluctant informants. Benjamin D. Paul has remarked that in the field "the anthropologist may think that he is making the choices, but in many instances it is equally true that the informants are choosing the anthropologist" (1953:443; also Nash 1963:149–67; Lowie 1959:59–62). Paul points out that the voluntary informant is almost per se outside the norm of his community—but the anthropologist, too, stands at the periphery of his own culture. The fieldworker and informant, both unusually willing to enter unfamiliar relationships and examine cultural expression at a slight distance from it, may themselves participate in a mediating subculture between the two parent cultures.

Paul isolates two categories of eagerly willing informants. One represents individuals who are deviant in the strict sense: individuals whose behavior has set them at odds with the community, which regards them as misfits and troublemakers. These, usually the first to offer assistance, can seriously hamper the collector's relationship with the community as a whole (Paul 1953:443–44). It is also true, although Paul passes over it, that such individuals are more likely to offer false, compromised, or useless material in return for the attention and importance of working with the collector. Frances Densmore, for example, recorded songs associated with the Sun Dance from a Sioux singer in the absence of her usual interpreter, Robert Higheagle. When Higheagle returned, he reported that the best singers would now have nothing to do with her, because the Sun Dance singer was known to be a murderer and a ne'er-do-well. Finally Densmore agreed to destroy the material collected from him, and the work continued unimpeded (Densmore [1917b] 1968:107). In this instance, there was apparently nothing wrong with the recordings themselves aside from the moral standing of the individual who had made them. Nevertheless, they could not be allowed to represent the community in her collection.

The other category of willing informants is represented by individuals whose standing in the community is good but who are by nature both more adventurous and more reflective than most. In the investigations carried out by collectors during the era of the cylinder phonograph, the cooperation of individuals of this second category was particularly important among Native Americans. Among Indians, especially those who had been Anglo-educated, there was a piercing awareness of the disappearance of the old ways no less genuine and painful for the fact that in the case of some aspects of traditional behavior their mourning was premature. Introduced in 1912, the *Society of American Indians Quarterly Journal* addressed all those committed to the advancement of Indians by means of gradual assimilation into Anglo-American society. The publication contained energetic exhortations from both whites and Indians for the documentation of traditional expressive manifestations such as song, narrative, and dance. Alanson B. Skinner, assistant curator of anthropology of the American Museum of Natural History, encouraged Indians to take the initiative themselves to collect and document their traditions in an article entitled "The Value of Recording Indian Folklore":

> Many of you do not know that there is a society—the American Folklore Society, whose object is to preserve these things among Americans [i.e., Indians] and whites in North America. This society would welcome your contributions and publish them, would be glad if you Americans would form local branches among your own people to record and preserve your lore. . . . Let us cooperate. Your secretary and I will be glad to help you to the end that American literature may no longer be unwritten, but take its place with the literature of Greece, Rome, Germany, England, Scandinavia, and France. (1915:48)

Indian contributions to the *Quarterly Journal* sounded similar appeals, insisting that Indian culture be evaluated in the same terms as ancient European civilizations, and at the same time celebrating progress on the road to assimilation with Anglo-American culture. Thus

Evelyn Two Guns's note entitled "The Indian Fondness for Music" enthuses over Indian participation in brass bands and in mandolin and guitar clubs, and observes that "on one Western reservation nearly every home has either a self-playing piano or a Victrola." She reports with pride that the government (probably meaning the BAE) has engaged in the collecting of traditional Indian music by means of the phonograph. In conclusion she expresses the hope that Indians will continue to broaden their appreciation of other musics and will cooperate with the efforts to preserve "the old tribal melodies" (1915:35–36).

Among Indians who were not fully committed to eventual assimilation, grief at the passing of the old way of life was bitterly keen, unmixed with optimism. Robert H. Lowie tells of taking a group of Crow and Blackfoot on a visit to the Bronx Zoo in 1907. One old Blackfoot stopped at the zoo's buffalo range and let the rest of the group go on to the other exhibits without him, while he remained rapt at a sight then gone from the ranges where his ancestors had hunted (Lowie 1959:50). For such individuals, appalled rather than enthralled by the prospect of an Indian future marched to the tune of brass bands and mandolin clubs, the phonograph offered the possibility of storing the old ways safely until such time as they might be wanted once more.

For those Indians urgently concerned with the preservation of their ceremonies, music, and language, the phonograph presented certain distinct advantages when used in a fieldwork encounter. This fact has been virtually ignored in the professional literature. Manuals and works on the practice of fieldwork even today tend to emphasize the negative aspects of mechanical documentation, warning that it makes informants self-conscious, is distracting, or creates an unnatural situation. Despite these problems, Georges and Jones comment, "According to fieldworkers' oral and published reports . . . surprising numbers of subjects readily agree or are easily persuaded to allow themselves to be taped or photographed. The reasons for this are not entirely clear" (1980:146). Actually, in the case of fieldwork encounters in the era of the cylinder phonograph, certain reasons *can* be adduced for their ready cooperation in the mechanical recording of ethnographic material. Far from being intimidated by the phonograph, many informants appear to have found it an acceptable, even welcome element in the fieldworker encounter—a dependable point of reference in what could be a personally and socially hazardous undertaking.

One reason for its welcome was its very newness. The phonograph was a novelty, especially in the initial years of its use, and for some individuals its use was, quite simply, fun. Helen Roberts recalled that some Jamaican singers would come from great distances to perform, and their excitement over the machine caused unexpected problems: "The records were not always satisfactory, since the people were quite unaccustomed to the phonograph. No one had ever seen one before. So great was their curiosity that it was almost impossible to keep them from pressing upon and shaking the table or chair in which the machine stood, or from singing too softly or too loudly. Such troubles all collectors will understand" (1925:155n1). Frances Densmore learned that an elusive Tohono O'odham singer refused to believe the reports he heard from acquaintances concerning the capabilities of the machine. She diplomatically invited him for a personal demonstration, and he was impressed enough to add to her collection himself. Though Cecil Sharp resented being beholden to a device he rather disliked, he believed he owed his life to the novelty of the phonograph, as exotic in the English countryside at the turn of the century as it was in the Sonora desert. In the midst of a session recording songs from a young Gypsy woman, the folksong collector heard the unexpected approach of her jealous husband. Sharp threw open the caravan door, and shouted, "A happy Christmas to you. Stop a moment and listen. I've got your wife's voice in a box." According to Maud Karpeles, "the man was so amazed and delighted he forgot to kill Cecil Sharp, and instead they became great friends" (1967:41).

From the standpoint of the performer, the phonograph was not merely fun but expedient. Ethnographers complain eloquently concerning the burdens and inconveniences of fieldwork, often forgetting that the task can be tedious and unrewarding to the subjects as well.

Once the unfamiliarity of the phonograph had worn off, the reaction most frequently reported among singers amounted to simple gratitude for a machine that obviated the performance of songs and tales over and over to a collector attempting to take a written transcription. Percy Grainger found that the use of the phonograph not only thrilled his rural English performers because of its novelty and convenience but also seemed to improve their performances, enhancing their sense of rhythmic and dynamic contrast and dramatic effect (1909:147). In the course of her fieldwork in Jamaica, Helen Heffron Roberts observed that when working with singers who found that tedious repetition made songs "souah to yo' mout'," the phonograph provided a welcome means of inducing cooperation (Roberts 1925:152; see also Wyman 1920:321–35).

It was not merely novelty and expedience that commended the phonograph to informants. The device offered a means of recording requiring, at least for the duration of the session, a real *collaboration* between the informant and collector mediated by the machine, the terms of which were negotiable. By refusing to work further with Frances Densmore unless she destroyed the Sun Dance recordings made by a community outcast, the Sioux exerted control through the recording process not only on Densmore's collecting but also on the group as a whole; unacceptable behavior disqualified one from employment—and payment—as a performer ([1917b] 1968:39–40). In his outmaneuvering Frances Densmore over the cylinder to be sent to the commissioner of Indian Affairs, the Ute chief Red Cap's faith in the efficacy of his own voice in persuading the commissioner calls attention to a second factor that commended the cylinder phonograph to informant cultures.

The collectors belonged to chirographic societies, not only literate but privileging the *written* document over the aural. Even the cylinder recordings were in most cases translated into musical and verbal transcriptions on paper before they were recognized as valid scholarly evidence. But among the cultures from which fieldworkers collected, the aural event often had primacy even when the informants were fully or nominally literate. Maud Karpeles reported that in the course of Cecil Sharp's 1916 trip in the southern Appalachians he showed an old singer the transcription of the song he had just performed. The singer remarked, "Well, I can't hardly recognize it" (Karpeles 1967:154). Francis La Flesche found that in order to discuss the meaning of ceremonies with Osage Saucy Calf, he had to use a combination of phonograph replay and memorization on his own part, as the old man could not abide hearing him read from written transcriptions (*Annual Report* 1912:38). An appreciation of recorded over written material is still characteristic of the Tohono O'odham, according to Ruth Underhill; while Papago ceremonies continue to be transcribed by Anglos, "for communication among themselves, the People prefer the tape recorder, which does away with writing" (1979a:96). In a sense, the tape recorder and cylinder phonograph offer to aurally oriented people the best of two worlds. A sound event is reproduced aurally note for note and nuance for nuance, and is contained, like a written document, in a concrete artifactual form that can be referred to again and again.

Ruth M. Stone has observed that among the Kpelle of Liberia, audial communication is so centrally valued that other kinds of experience are habitually translated in terms of sound in order to convey meaning (Stone 1981:188–206). In her use of the "feedback interview," in which researcher and Kpelle participants review the playback of a completed event in order to evaluate it and reconstruct its meaning, Stone has highly refined and specialized a procedure that, in very rudimentary form, is virtually as old as the mechanical recording of performances: the custom of playing back the record just made for the performer. Whether the medium for playback is videotape or cylinder recording, inference on the part of the collector is reduced when re-creation of the event from notes is not required (Stone 1982:52–54).

In the era of the cylinder phonograph, collectors generally considered this procedure no more than a means of checking the quality of the recording and pleasing the participant, neglecting to record the commentary unless it was particularly amusing or unusual. As far as they were concerned, the significant event began when the cylinder rolled and concluded when the cylinder came to an end. Evidence suggests, however, that this playback served an important function for the informant, giving the performer an opportunity to validate the quality and accuracy of the performance and to verify that, indeed, the voice was preserved permanently in the wax in a form that could not be altered without destroying the whole: a speaking object that would be, as the collector promised, preserved in a house that would not burn.

For those informants who took the preservation of traditional materials seriously as a privilege and a duty, the chance to review the performance even briefly was a valued opportunity. Ruth Underhill found that her Papago informants were reluctant to correct her written phonetic transcriptions when they heard them read back, for fear that their criticism of her skill as a transcriber would hurt her feelings, but no such considerations applied to correction of material recorded by the phonograph (1979b:33). Concerning her singers' satisfaction with the machine, Helen Heffron Roberts recalled:

> I remember there was one man singing me a song, and he had a way of ending it up, but he changed it constantly. . . . He was a man I was very much interested in. He had a whole lot of stuff. He could give you almost any kind of flourish, as he called them. A flourish on this and a flourish on that. But he was beyond me because he changed this flourish every time. . . . Finally I got disgusted. . . . and I said, "When we get the phonograph, I'll have you come and take it down, we'll get it down again." So the phonograph finally came. I started the phonograph and went through, and of course it got everything, and I played it back for him. "Ahhh, Missy! the little box got all the flourishes." (Roberts 1979)

Not only did the phonograph spare the informant the awkwardness of correcting the collector directly, it also offered the opportunity for the informant to correct himself. Katcora, a Yuma of Arizona who energetically assisted Frances Densmore in 1922 by scouting potential singers and accompanying them to Fort Yuma Agency to be recorded, wished to conclude his work with her by recording a formal speech. As he spoke no English, the address was recorded in Yuman, with Densmore's interpreter translating. Katcora expressed his approval of Densmore's work and announced the conclusion of his own participation, naming the date and hour of the morning. The record was played back, and Katcora was seized with a sudden doubt concerning the accuracy of the time he had given. Watches were compared; the discrepancy was a matter of fifteen minutes. Katcora was deeply distressed, and insisted that another record be made in which his statement of time would be correct.[7]

The phonograph not only enabled performers to verify the quality of their performance, it enabled them to include statements not intrinsically part of the performance that would, they hoped, protect them from any untoward consequences stemming from their participation. Melville and Frances Herskovits's informants in Surinam were unwilling to assist in the writing down of song texts, apparently concerned that such action might be misinterpreted by supernatural powers. The anthropologists found, on the other hand, that most of their informants were quite willing to sing for the phonograph because they could preface their performances with an explanation of their motives addressed to their ancestors and personal spirits, and further protect themselves by misnaming the pieces (Herskovits and Herskovits 1936:525).

A gracious expression of approval extended to some ethnographers and their recording machines may be found in the phenomenon of songs composed to be recorded that are about the recording process. These compositions, reflecting the event from the point of view of the singer, represent interesting exercises in formulation and expression of attitudes and images concerning the phonograph itself and the ethnographic encounter. The Karok singer Fritz Hansen had composed a Kick Dance song about his first encounter with the phonograph, which he sang some years later for Helen H. Roberts's machine as an example of how anything might become the subject of a song. In a concise three lines it remarks on the phonograph's ability to replay singing right away, as though a man were within it:

> getting ready first him talk
> getting ready to sing
> iron in he is singing.[8]

Roberts also collected a name chant composed by the Hawaiian singer Minnie Lovell, which translated runs in part:

> This song praises the flower of America,
> The flower from the icy cold of California
> You are anointed by the touring star.
> Searching for the hidden riddles of Hawai'i,
> The beautiful chants of long ago.
>
> I love my companion,
> From this foreign land.
> You search for wisdom,
> With the machine that picks up the voice.
> (Roberts 1980)

From the anecdotes and fragmentary accounts related by collectors who themselves were often uncertain or unaware of their meaning, a complex picture emerges. Compliance on the part of informants could by no means be taken for granted; it was a matter of choice shaped by a number of factors. Social pressures sometimes inhibited potential informants. Economic or official pressure could induce cooperation, as could desire to extend courtesy to a guest or placate someone with power. Some embraced the opportunity to record despite inconvenience and even danger because of a deep desire to preserve materials they considered sacred and endangered by time. The phonograph provided a means of documenting performances in a social context that contained elements of a true collaboration, producing a product—the cylinder record—that fulfilled the agendas of both collector and informant.

For those to whom preservation of traditional material was a sacred mission, participation in the recording process could represent a sacrament in itself. Ki-ri-ki'-ri-su re-ka'-wa-ri, or Running Scout, a Pawnee priest, visited Washington, D.C., in the company of the BAE ethnologist James Murie, himself Pawnee. Murie encouraged the old man to record the details of the Hako ceremony for Alice C. Fletcher at her home. According to her notes, this prospect troubled him until he received supernatural encouragement:

On Saturday morning, November 30, 1901, Running Scout came up to my study with a smiling face, the expression of trouble which had been so marked all the week seem[ed] to have gone. Mr. James Murie remarked, "The old man is happy this morning. He says that he had a dream last night, I know he waked me up singing, and he has been singing again this morning."

Later Running Scout said to me, "I have been waiting for a sign from Ti-ra-wa as to my telling you about these sacred things, last night it was given to me. I know now that it is all right now for me to speak to you."

After lunch, Running Scout again came to my study with clean clothing on and his face freshly painted. He was always neat and his hair smooth and glossy, parted in the middle and the locks bound into stiff, long rolls with a strip of green woolen cloth, hung down on each shoulder. I learned that he had taken a bath, put on clean raiment throughout, and had thus made himself ready for the singing of the sacred songs.

It was an exhausting task for the ailing singer, but he persisted, referring to the horn of the phonograph as the pipe he was lifting in honor of Ti-ra-wa. The demand on his emotions was immense:

Running Scout had finished telling of the lodge where[in] the ceremonies were to take place and the offering of the buffalo tongue and heart to be made, when he broke into ungovernable weeping. When he recovered sufficiently to speak, he said,

"I am thinking of the disappearance of the buffalo, of all the animals which Ti-ra-wa made for us to live by and with which to worship him. We can no longer make sacrifice to Ti-ra-wa a-ti-us, we can no longer obey his injunctions, we can no longer live by the food which he bade us to use. I seem to stand on the edge of a high place, where everything is behind me, and there is no place to stand or walk in the future. My heart is very heavy, I cannot help but weep.

"It is very strange that I am here. I have told you how when I was a little boy and when I was a young man I lived with the old men that I might learn of these sacred things. My grandfather taught me of the bundle which is now in my keeping, and he told me how it had come down to our time and how its ceremonies were to be kept. My grandfather died, many things happened, our tribe was removed from our old home in Nebraska, the buffalo and the game have been exterminated, much trouble has come to all of us and much trouble has come to me. I was very severely wounded when we were attacked by the Sioux, I lost an eye, and was very sick, for I hurt internally. I have lived, I hardly know how, but it must be for some purpose. I have been thinking about that. I have been wondering how is has come about that you and I are here together, talking about these things. I am not here of my own will or my planning. I think it has been brought about by Ti-ra-wa. He must have put in your heart the desire to preserve these ceremonies of my people which are now no longer performed. That has become impossible. It must have been Ti-ra-was who pointed me out to you as the one, the only one who is now living who knows these sacred songs and their meaning, and to you to send for me. He had a purpose in it.

"It was to the woman that Ti-ra-wa first spoke of these things, and now it is again to a woman of the white race that he speaks and tells her whom she is to ask, that she may learn about these things. I have been thinking about this, and now that it has been shown to me that Ti-ra-wa has brought about this meeting between you and me I am feeling easier. I am not so troubled in speaking to you of these sacred things. I think it was Ti-ra-wa directed you where to search for me, and now that you have found me and I am here, having come this long journey to meet you, I think it is Ti-ra-wa's will that I should give you this knowledge which I have long held, buried in my heart.

"You say you will preserve it, so that it will never be lost. That is right. You say that you will not let it be desecrated. That is right. What you say is right and makes me glad. I will remember your words."[9]

The horn of the phonograph becomes, in the old man's eyes, a manifestation of the sacred pipe: he breathes and, through the work of his breath in a manmade tool, something holy lives on.

5

A Spiral Way
Bringing the Voices Home

> I feel there is much to be said for the Celtic belief that the souls of those whom we have lost are held captive in some inferior being, in an animal, in a plant, in some inanimate object, and so effectively lost to us until the day (which for some never comes) when we happen to pass by the tree or to obtain possession of the object which forms their prison. Then they start and tremble, they call us by our name, and as soon as we have recognized their voice, the spell is broken. We have delivered them: they have overcome death and returned to share our life.
>
> *Marcel Proust, Swann's Way*

The modest Capitol Hill row house where Running Scout recorded for Alice Fletcher was razed in the mid-1970s to make way for the James Madison Building, part of the Library of Congress—coincidentally, the very building that would eventually house her cylinder collections and those of her adopted Omaha son, Francis La Flesche. I first encountered the Fletcher and La Flesche cylinders in 1981, in a chilly recording studio tucked deep in the fin-de-siècle Beaux-Arts extravagance of the Jefferson Building, just across Independence Avenue.

The vividness of the voices they preserved astonished me. The recordings had less surface noise than most and were exceptionally free from damage and distortion, but it was not so much what the cylinders lacked that struck me, it was what was *there,* surviving years of neglect–a kind of freshness of presence enabling the listener to imagine not only the singers but the setting, evoking the clarity of light and the quality of the air. I had seen an old photograph of a powwow arena and a grove of oak trees on the Omaha reservation at

Macy, Nebraska, where gatherings were held and some of these songs must have been sung–but my job was rerecording the cylinders, not musing about their past. I dutifully dispatched the voices in the wax to their places on tape, interspersing each cut with my own identification announcements and technical remarks, and went on to the next batch of cylinders, an unwitting and unlikely newcomer to Running Scout's band of women preserving tradition.

Tribal representatives and delegations regularly visit Washington today just as they have done for the last two hundred years. As word got out concerning the cylinder project, the Library of Congress became a routine stop on their itinerary. In the spring of 1983, Dennis Hastings, the Omaha tribal archivist, called on the Cylinder Project team. Project director Dorothy Sara Lee brought Hastings to the lab so that I could show him the cylinders and play some of the Omaha material. He listened with motionless intensity, his excitement clear. Folklife Center staff had already been thinking about producing an album of the Omaha material with accompanying notes, but it was Hastings's enthusiasm that sparked this plan to life.

His visit was timely. As the preservation phase of the cylinder project was approaching completion, the staff was looking for models for its final phase of the project, a two-year initiative in which copies of cylinder recordings and related documentary material would be returned to the American Indian tribes from which they had been originally recorded. Seemingly straightforward, this objective posed many delicate problems of ethics and diplomacy: as has been seen, the circumstances under which recordings had been obtained were sometimes questionable, and some of the material was sacred and highly sensitive (Brady et al. 1984:18). Clearly, the return of the cylinders needed careful attention on a tribe-by-tribe basis, with as much advice, assistance, and collaboration as possible from members of each group.

Dorothy Lee was scheduled to return precious archival tapes of the Fletcher and La Flesche Omaha recordings at the Omaha annual powwow in September of 1983. To make a sampler of these recordings even more accessible, Hastings proposed that the Folklife Center coproduce an album with the Omaha Tribal Council, and that the release of the album coincide with the 1985 powwow, where the music would be welcomed home by the Tribal Council, members of the Hethu'shka Society, and the Omaha people. The Folklife Center would be represented by director Alan Jabbour, Cylinder Project director Dorothy Sara Lee, and me. I was to see the arena in the grove of oaks after all.

I arrived to find the celebration in its second day, already in full swing. In the half-light behind the risers that defined the arena the immense, gaudy-feathered headdresses and bustles worn by the fancy dancers glared as though they had an inner source of light. The bells attached to the leggings of the costumed men made a steadily pulsing, high-pitched shivery noise like a field of crickets. It sounded disconcertingly like surface noise on a cylinder; somewhere at the back of my mind I kept searching for the sound's frequency, as though I could reach for a dial and edit it away. It took a while before I could not only accept it but enjoy it.

The overload of alterations and continuities was confounding. It was bewildering to walk at early evening in the shade of the very trees I had seen in the old photo, and bewildering to hear the songs that I had heard before thinly rendered on wax now shake the air and throb the ground beneath my feet. The influence of the recordings returned in 1983 was evident both in repertoire and style. Dorothy Lee's fieldnotes concur, observing that "something *had* happened . . . the songs *are* stronger, and the Omaha seem more confident, perhaps seeing themselves reflected in attention from the outside world."

The dancing and singing were continuous and compelling. Dennis reminded us that we would be expected to dance, as well, on Sunday during our honoring song. There were half a dozen clowns, male and female, scattered among the dancers, whom Clifford Wolf, the emcee, referred to with glee as visitors from Washington from the renowned BIA tribe. I prayed that we would acquit ourselves as dancers acceptably if not with honor, and that Omaha powwows to come would not include a comic contingent from the long lost AFC tribe, like the Zuni send-up of Jesse Walter Fewkes. My observation of the women dancers took on a desperate intensity.

Sunday's events began for us with a lunchtime feast given by Charlie Holt on behalf of the Hethu'shka Society and attended by members of the society and their families. We sat in a circle on a windy hillside by an abandoned Mormon church and ate our fill. Then, led by Hollis Stabler, one by one the men of the society stood and spoke to us of the meaning of the recordings that we had a part in bringing back to Macy, and the meaning for them of the songs of the past in making one's way now as an Omaha. Many echoed the feelings expressed by Dennis Hastings in the liner notes he had written for the album we were about to present:

> When I hear the cylinders, they lead to thoughts about what songs were still alive and what songs we had lost. . . . They managed to survive this long and to go back to the people. I think that now we have them we will never lose them again. . . . If you listen to the words of them, they mean involvement with nature and our being and our surroundings. It's a tie, a connection to every living thing–man's power of growth and movement, the ability to think, to will, and to bring to pass. . . .
>
> We shall not be false to any great truths that have been revealed to us concerning the world in which we live, if we listen to the olden voice, an unseen heritage of our bounteous land, as it sings of our unity with nature. That's what I mean by the tie. Without that we have broken the circles of nature itself, which flows in one circular motion.
>
> I didn't know quite what to expect when the songs on the cylinders came back. After a year or so now it has affected people in different ways. For some of the older singers and older people that remember those songs, it is renewing, it brightens them up, because it supports what they have been saying and standing for all along. During the last pow-wow the singers started singing songs that no one had heard before. It was like a supernatural or spiritual gift that had been given back to the people again. (Hastings 1985:1–2)

Seated at Dennis's side on that Nebraska hillside, I thought of the many tedious hours spent in that back studio over the course of almost a decade of watching the mandrel spin endless spirals of cylinder grooves past the phonograph's needle. And how a job that seems just a way to make ends meet and get from one point to another professionally can sometimes become something more, linking you with larger continuities, spirals, and circles than you know. We returned to the powwow arena, itself a great circle with the drum at the heart. Alan presented a copy of the album to singer Charlie Edwards, we each spoke our thanks to the assembly, and we took our place in the dance.

Figure 5.1. Omaha powwow, 1985; Macy, Nebraska. Charlie Edwards receives copy of *Omaha Indian Music* from American Folklife Center director Alan Jabbour, as Erika Brady, technical consultant; Dorothy Sara Lee, Federal Cylinder Project director; and Dennis Hastings, archivist and tribal historian, look on. Library of Congress.

Writing in 1936, George Herzog estimated that more than fourteen thousand cylinder recordings of North American traditional materials had been made between 1890 and 1935. Most of these cylinders survive today, preserving hundreds of hours of music, ceremony, and narrative, some of which remain documented only in this form. In the creation of this legacy, the phonograph was an essential tool: as many collectors acknowledged, the sheer volume of material recorded could not have been achieved without technical assistance.

But the cylinder phonograph was more than a means to accomplish the collectors' intentions efficiently and effectively. As we have seen in instances such as Densmore's confrontation with Red Cap and

Fletcher's recording sessions with Running Scout, the phonograph represented a means to mediate the differences of purpose that separated collector and informant. It produced an object, the wax cylinder, that was truly an impartial record of a sound event, verifiable by both performer and collector. In a sense, even its technical limitations had a certain useful function: any direct request or demand made by a collector of an informant was fraught with the complications imposed by the curious subordinate/insubordinate role negotiations surrounding the collecting of fieldwork. The presence of the phonograph could not eliminate these tensions, but it appears in instances such as those sketched in the previous chapter to have eased them to a surprising extent. The use of the phonograph created a context in which both the collector and informant collaborated in order to respond effectively to the technical demands of the machine, resulting in a product for which both could claim responsibility. Although the collector took the recordings away, the performer could nevertheless regard the collector's role as custodial: the cylinders would now be protected in Washington in a house that would never burn, until they were called upon to speak again to a generation who perhaps would be more responsive to their message. A material object separate from both the collector and the performer, the mechanically produced cylinder recording could survive them both, and survive as well the often mistaken theoretical assumptions and misguided personal agendas that bound their thinking, to take on a new set of meanings and uses decades later. How could Alice Fletcher have foreseen the events in Macy in 1985?

The enduring importance of this legacy of recording has long been recognized by scholars. The ethnologists who took the machines to the field carried the recordings back as evidence of their participation in traditions of scholarship already well established by the time the phonograph became available. In recent decades, however, the value of these recordings to the descendants of the performers has become more and more dramatically apparent; the cylinders have begun to fulfill in part the intentions of their native creators. Those performers who shared their traditions in the subversive hope that they would be a valued legacy to their descendants have been vindicated. Ironically, the Federal Cylinder Project undertook to collaborate with tribal groups to make available materials originally collected in order to preserve music, ritual, and languages that federal policy at the time of their recording had intended to drive into the ground within a generation.

Nor has the value of the cylinder recordings been limited to American Indian communities. In 1980, residents of the area surrounding Old Mines, Missouri, petitioned the Federal Cylinder Project with hundreds of signatures to make available to them recordings of French cylinders made in the region by Joseph Médard Carrière in the mid-thirties, stating "these materials are vital to our own cultural study projects, and it is important for us to obtain them now, while we can still learn more about their background and context from people who remember hearing these things themselves" (Brady et al. 1984:18). In the course of my own later fieldwork in Old Mines, I discovered to my surprise that, although the Carrière cylinders themselves proved to be in a state of deterioration that made retrieval of their content almost impossible, the mere circumstance of their return to the community and the attention given them stimulated local awareness, reviving interest in the region's French heritage. This process of reintroduction of lost or forgotten materials into communities through initiatives such as the Federal Cylinder Project raises its own set of issues, material for further dialogue concerning preservation and representation of culture both within a community and by outside agencies and individuals (Vennum 1984; Baron and Spitzer 1992; Cantwell 1993; Kurin 1997).

The era of the cylinder phonograph ended some fifty years ago. Smaller and more sensitive devices for recording aural and visual data create new methodological and ethical dilemmas, while they expand fieldwork possibilities. New technological advances offer a siren promise of virtual re-creation of the sense impressions of a moment, unimpeded by any obvious mechanical presence and seemingly unfiltered by the ethnographic eye. But as we riddle our way through these new technologies, we may be sure that the dynamics of the basic human encounter will remain–the complex cross-cultural give-and-take in which individuals from different worlds negotiate roles and fulfill objectives in an atmosphere of exhilaration and tension. The issues faced by the ethnographers of the cylinder era are still our own: the challenge to reconcile role-playing with reality, courtesy with mission.

The cylinders remain, like the magical objects dreamed of by Proust that, revived as though by sorcery, "start and tremble, and call us by name." Voices of men and women long dead speak from their grooves. To those who care to learn the limitations and possibilities of the process, and the complicated motives that led collector and informant to their strange meetings with the machine, these voices still speak truly, as the performers meant. Recorded by Caoimhín Ó Danachair, the Irishman Tomás Ó Crohan spoke of the spiraling path of their cry across time and space: "It is not now as it was then, but it is like a sea on ebb, and only pools here and there left among the rocks. And it is a good thought of us to put down the songs and stories before they are lost from the world forever. For the like of us will never be seen again."

Notes

1. As will be seen in chapter 3, it is not clear whether the honor of being the first individual to make ethnographic field recordings in fact belongs to Fewkes, as is usually assumed. He was, however, the first to publicize the potential of the phonograph as a field tool; see Fewkes 1890b, 1890c, and 1890d.

CHAPTER 1

1. Read and Welch 1958:14.

2. Other inventors were hot on Edison's heels in the invention of a mechanical device for recording sound, notably Charles Cros, whose concept for such a device, untested, was submitted to the Académie des Sciences de France in April 1877 (Read and Welch 1959:6–7). Edison's preeminence remains unchallenged; the other contenders serve to demonstrate that the idea of such a device was very much a part of the atmosphere of the era.

CHAPTER 2

1. Mach is now perhaps best remembered as the eponym of the number beloved of sci-fi writers representing the ratio of speed of an object to the speed of sound ("Approaching Mach One!"). Later we shall see how his provocative programmatic writings proposed a radical critical positivism in all the sciences that deeply influenced a generation of American ethnologists of the Boasian school, particularly Robert Lowie, and that indirectly shaped their use of the phonograph as an ethnographic tool.

2. The experiments supporting the hypotheses of top-down processing were primarily organized to evaluate visual perception; its application to other senses was generalized from that data. Then and since, phenomenology of vision has been most extensively explored of all the senses. Sight lends itself most readily of all the sense modalities to empirical investigation, but even aside from its conveniently measurable characteristics, its preeminence would have been virtually guaranteed by the privileged role given sight among the senses in Western

European society, representing the legacy of Immanuel Kant's division of the senses into "higher" (sight, hearing), and lower (smell, touch, taste) domains (Stoller 1989:8–9).

The faculty of hearing, though supposedly but a step below sight as a so-called rational and aesthetic "higher" sense, has not had a proportionate share in these careful experimental investigations and speculations. The preeminence of sight is explored from a folkloristic standpoint in Dundes 1980.

3. Cited in *Phonogram* 4, no. 5 (March 1902): 77. A number of references in this chapter are to three trade journals published by Thomas A. Edison's network of phonograph companies for their distributors, jobbers, and retail salesmen. These publications included descriptions of newly released commercial recordings, sales pep talks, promotional ideas, news of recent technical developments, and diatribes against rival companies' products. Most important of all for the purposes of this chapter, they also reprinted articles appearing in newspapers concerning the phonograph. Unless otherwise noted, references in this chapter are to newspaper articles quoted and paraphrased in these magazines. Unfortunately, no information aside from the name of the newspaper is given, and sometimes the newspaper is alluded to only by location. It is impossible, therefore, to verify these citations at the source.

Hereafter, *Phonogram* will be abbreviated *Ph, New Phonogram* as *NPh,* and *Edison Phonograph Monthly* as *EPM.*

4. The role of the urban legend in a society's adaptation to a new technology is explored in Brunvand 1981:62–65. Use of urban legend to stigmatize communities with marginal status is investigated in Baer 1982. An interesting and germane example of the marriage between popular reaction to a technological innovation and preexistent elements common in oral tradition can be found in Allen 1982.

5. The episode represents an early example of "playing the Whiteman," a widespread joking behavior among American Indians brilliantly documented in Basso 1979.

6. According to Stith Thompson's comprehensive system of folktale plot elements, the phonograph corresponds to Thompson Motif D 1610, "Magic speaking object." Related motifs include D 1610.21, "Speaking image," and D 1620, "Magic automata" (Thompson 1955–58).

7. A brief account of "anomalous" ethnographic cylinder recordings—those made in the course of fieldwork to test or demonstrate the machine—in one major archival collection can be found in Cassell 1984.

8. The "original" Nipper, model for the painting by Francis Barraud, had belonged to the artist's brother, Mark Henry Barraud. The artist took the terrier on his master's death in 1887. Many anecdotes concerning the dog were related by Francis Barraud after the painting had made them both famous, but none allude to any confusion over the dead brother's voice on record, and the story concerning the phantom coffin in the background of an early version of the painting appears to have no foundation (Petts 1983:n.p.).

CHAPTER 3

1. Composed by the ethnologist in 1922, in honor of C. Hart Merriam. In the early 1980s, ethnomusicologist Judith Gray set this post-Victorian ode to the tune of Felix Mendelssohn's "Consolation" from *Songs Without Words* (third song, book 2, opus 30), whereupon for a time it became the unofficial anthem of the Federal Cylinder Project.

2. It is possible that one of the "others" who had suggested the use of the phonograph was Mary Hemenway herself. Her role in promoting early fieldwork in the study of Indian music and ceremony and her specific contributions to their recording on cylinder has never been fully appreciated. Of the 158 extant field recordings in Frank Gillis's list of ethnographic fieldwork "incunabula" dating from the first five years in which the phonograph was available, Mary Hemenway's financial backing had supported 141 (1984). Her death in 1894 brought to a close the first stage in the use of the phonograph in fieldwork—a period dominated by the efforts of Fewkes and Benjamin Ives Gilman, whose work she also supported.

Although she is primarily remembered as a generous supporter of early ethnological research and other philanthropic endeavor, it is less well-known that she was a major shareholder in the Edison Phonograph Company and a key figure in the agreement between Edison and Jesse Lippincott that enabled the commercial production of the phonograph to proceed in 1888 (Read and Welch 1959:40). It seems likely that her financial involvement with the infant recording industry had some bearing on the use of the machine in her ethnological field expeditions. Even if the initial suggestion for the use of the phonograph in such work lay elsewhere, Mrs. Hemenway probably facilitated the acquisition of machines for collectors during the years in which under normal circumstances a full year's expensive lease was required.

3. The fieldwork dilemma of "profitability" versus "sociability" as competing values is explored in Jackson 1989:156–69.

4. Inventories of the material holdings of the BAE were published each year in the *Annual Report of the Board of Regents of the Smithsonian Institution.*

5. The influence of William James on more recent folklore scholarship through the work of George Herbert Mead is discussed in Bronner 1990.

Boas's reluctance to pronounce on collected data is a persistent leitmotif in critical accounts of his influence. Marion Smith strikes a typically exasperated tone: "The exhaustive collection of data which seems at the time to have little or no connection with any specific problem is peculiarly a feature of [Boas's] approach....Masses of data may therefore be worked over with no clear knowledge of what's to be gained at the end. A new hypothesis or a new slant on an old problem will "emerge" or be "revealed" or "suggested." The data will "speak for themselves....Boas was always too self-critical to rely completely on his own observations. He needed the documentation of the texts, the family history, to test his own precision" (1959:54–56).

6. He remarked much later with regard to Frances Densmore's work, "the study of form is not easy, because in transcriptions made from the phonograph—and I presume that most of the material in Miss Densmore's book has been so transcribed—accents are not reliable, because mechanically accents are introduced on those tones that correspond to the rate of vibration of the diaphragm" (Boas 1925:319).

7. The Pearson Circle was one of several memorable discussion groups established by Goldenweiser, a popular and charismatic student at Columbia, that were modeled on groups formed in Russian universities to study the emerging topics in psychology, philosophy, and history of sciences. The circle was named for Karl Pearson, author of the influential *Grammar of Sciences* (Deacon 1997:99–101).

8. An excellent discussion of the intellectual climate of the early years of anthropology at Columbia can be found in Deacon 1997:97–107.

9. The description "systematic self-professionalization" is Robert Lowie's (1943:183).

10. The topic of Boas's non-evolutionary orientation toward the past, and its implications in his concern with the evidential value of texts, is explored in Stocking 1974:85–86. Stocking further explores the implications of this stance in relation to his approach to linguistics and his work with the BAE in Stocking 1992:89–91; see also Hymes 1970.

11. A partial list of collectors sponsored by the BAE who made use of the phonograph includes John Wight Chapman, Frances Densmore, Alice Cunningham Fletcher, Leo Joachim Frachtenberg, John Peabody Harrington, John N. P. Hewitt, Melville Jacobs, Herbert Krieger, Francis La Flesche, Thurlow Lieurance, Truman Michelson, James Murie, Paul Radin, Maurice Greer Smith, Matthew Stirling, and John Swanton.

12. A discussion of Cecil Sharp's dislike of the phonograph both as collecting tool and as cultural force is offered in Karpeles 1967:34, 41.

13. It might also be argued that women ethnographers were unencumbered by what appears to have been a peculiarly male rejection of the use of technical equipment as an impediment to their self-image as an assimilated participant in the life of the community—in Freilich's terms, a "marginal native" (1970). Although women in the field often established warm and even intimate relationships with community members, especially other women, they seldom displayed the rather adolescent overidentification that resulted in embarrassing photographs of male anthropologists in loincloths, squatting over tinder and flint.

CHAPTER 4

1. Translated some years later, Red Cap's cylinder did not include a scathing indictment against the agent as Densmore feared but rather a message of approval concerning Densmore's activities and a plea to the Commissioner to allow the Utes free participation in the pastimes and religious ceremonies of their tradition; possibly the agent in question had interfered with these activities. The original transcript is in the National Anthropological Archives; a photocopy is in the files of the Federal Cylinder Project, American Folklife Center, Library of Congress. Two personal memoirs of this episode survive: a formal report sent to the BAE archives and reprinted in Hofmann 1968:39–43, and a typescript dated 6 June 1943 containing a somewhat more detailed and circumstantial account. A photocopy of the latter version is in the files of the Federal Cylinder Project, American Folklife Center, Library of Congress; the original is in the National Anthropological Archives,

Smithsonian Institution. In addition, Hofmann reprints a letter from Densmore to her sister, Margaret Densmore, briefly recounting the event on the evening it occurred, 16 July 1914 (1968:35–37).

2. Indian rights advocate D. A. Goddard, editor of the *Boston Daily Advertiser*, in 1886 wrote contemptuously of Alice Cunningham Fletcher's "wretchedly sentimental way of calling the Omaha her children—her babies—and such pet names" (Mark 1988:107).

3. This story still circulates orally among folklorists and anthropologists working for the federal government, sometimes attaching itself to Frances Densmore.

4. Ironically, John A. Lomax is better known for arranging the release of Huddie Ledbetter (Leadbelly) from Angola Prison, although he was not in fact responsible; the musician's time was reduced for good behavior, and not in response to any intervention on Lomax's part (Porterfield 1996:529n6).

5. The ethnographer's dilemma when negative consequences are imputed to a performer's cooperation in fieldwork remains a problem today, as Barre Toelken's wrenching discussion of his ongoing relationship with the family of Yellowman demonstrates (1998).

6. See, for example, Goldstein 1964:117; Farrer 1976:59–63; Diamond 1964:119–54.

7. Typescript memoir dated 18 June 1943 in National Anthropological Archives; photocopy in files of the Federal Cylinder Project, American Folklife Center, Library of Congress.

8. Helen Heffron Roberts Collection of Karok and Konimihu Indian Music, AFS no. 19,874–19,882. Archive of Folk Culture, American Folklife Center, Library of Congress.

9. This version of the episode is from the fragmentary typewritten notes kept by Fletcher, photocopies of which are in the files of the Federal Cylinder Project, American Folklife Center, Library of Congress. Drawing on these notes, Fletcher published the following paraphrase of Running Scout's summary of their work together in her published account "The Hako: A Pawnee Ceremony":

> As I have worked here day and night, my heart has gone out to you. I have done what has never been done before, I have given you all the

songs of this ceremony and explained them to you. I never thought that I, of all my people, should be the one to give this ancient ceremony to be preserved, and I wonder over it as I sit here.

I think over my long life with its many experiences; of the great number of Pawnees who have been with me in war, nearly all of whom have been killed in battle. I have been severely wounded many times—see this scar over my eye. I was with those who went to the Rocky Mountains to the Cheyennes, when so many soldiers were slain that their dead bodies lying there looked like a great blue blanket spread over the ground. When I think of all the people of my own tribe who have died during my lifetime and then of those in other tribes that have fallen by our hands, they are so many they make a vast cover over Mother Earth. I once walked with these prostrate forms. I did not fall but I passed on, wounded sometimes but not to death, until I am here today doing this thing, singing these sacred songs into that great pipe (the graphophone) and telling you of these ancient rites of my people. It must be that I have been preserved for this purpose, otherwise I would be lying back there among the dead. (Fletcher 1905:277–78)

References

Allen, Barbara. 1982. "The `Image on Glass': Technology, Tradition, and the Emergence of Folklore." *Western Folklore* 41:85–103.

Annual Report to the Board of Regents of the Smithsonian Institution for the Year 1911. 1912. Washington, D.C.: Government Printing Office.

Bacon, Alice Mabel. 1898. "Work and Methods of the Hampton Folk-Lore Society." *Journal of American Folk-Lore* 11:17–21.

Baer, Florence E. 1982. "`Give me...your huddled masses': Anti-Vietnamese Refugee Lore and the `Image of Limited Good.'" *Western Folklore* 41:275–91.

Barbeau, C-Marius. 1919. "The Field of European Folk-Lore in America." *Journal of American Folklore* 32:184–97.

Barnard, F. M., ed. and trans. 1969. *Herder on Social and Political Culture*. Cambridge: Cambridge University Press.

Baron, Robert, and Nicholas R. Spitzer. 1992. *Public Folklore*. Washington, D.C.: Smithsonian Institution Press.

Bartók, Béla. 1950. Liner notes, *Hungarian Folk Songs*. Folkways FE 4000.

Basso, Keith. 1979. *Portraits of "The Whiteman": Linguistic Play and Cultural Symbols Among the Western Apache*. Cambridge: Cambridge University Press.

Bayliss, Clara Kern. 1908. "Philippine Folk-Tales." *Journal of American Folklore* 21:46–63

Bird, Junius, and J. M. Tanner. 1953. "Technical Aids in Anthropology." In *An Appraisal of Anthropology Today*, ed. Alfred L. Kroeber, 191–217. Chicago: University of Chicago Press.

Bleuler, Eugen. 1950. *Dementia Praecox, or the Group of Schizophrenias*, trans. Joseph Zinkin. New York: International Universities Press.

Bloom, Lansing B., ed. 1936. "Bourke on the Southwest." *New Mexico Historical Review* 11:203–4.

Boas, Franz. [1889a] 1974. "The Aims of Ethnology." In *Die Ziele der Ethnologie*, 17–24. New York: Hermann Bartsch. Reprinted in *The Shaping of American Anthropology: A Franz Boas Reader*, ed. George W. Stocking, 1–20. New York: Basic Books.

———. [1889b] 1974. "On Alternating Sounds." *American*

Anthropologist 2:47–53. Reprinted in *The Shaping of American Anthropology: A Franz Boas Reader,* ed. George W. Stocking, 72–77. New York: Basic Books.

———. 1925. "Note: Teton Sioux Music." *Journal of American Folklore* 28:319.

Brady, Erika. 1988. "The Bureau of American Ethnology: Folklore, Fieldwork, and the Federal Government in the Late Nineteenth and Early Twentieth Centuries." In *The Conservation of Culture: Folklorists and the Public Sector,* ed. Burt Feintuch, pp. 35–45. Lexington: University Press of Kentucky.

Brady, Erika, et al. 1984. Introduction and Inventory. Vol. 1 of *The Federal Cylinder Project: A Guide to Field Cylinder Collections in Federal Agencies,* Dorothy Sara Lee, gen. ed. Studies in American Folklife, no. 3:1. Washington, D.C.: American Folklife Center, Library of Congress.

Brandes, Raymond Stewart. 1965. "Frank Hamilton Cushing: Pioneer Americanist." Ph.D. dissertation, University of Arizona.

Bronner, Simon J. 1986. *American Folklore Studies: An Intellectual History*. Lawrence: University Press of Kansas.

———. 1990. "'Toward a Common Center': Pragmatism and Folklore Studies." *Folklore Historian* 7:23–30.

Brunvand, Jan Harold. 1981. *The Vanishing Hitchhiker: American Urban Legends and Their Meanings.* New York: Norton.

"Bureau of American Ethnology." 1917. In *Annual Report of the Board of Regents of the Smithsonian Institution for the Year 1916,* 59–60. Washington, D.C.: Government Printing Office.

Cantwell, Robert. 1993. *Ethnomimesis: Folklife and the Representation of Culture.* Chapel Hill: University of North Carolina Press.

Carpenter, Edmund. 1972. *Oh What a Blow That Phantom Gave Me.* New York: Holt, Rinehart, and Winston.

Carpenter, Inta Gale. 1978. "Introspective Accounts of the Field Experience: A Bibliographic Essay." *Folklore Forum* 11:204–10.

Carterette, Edward C., and Morton P. Friedman, ed. 1978. *Hearing.* Vol. 4 of *Handbook of Perception.* New York: Academic Press.

Cassell, Nancy A. 1984. "Ethnographic Anomalies in Cylinder Recordings." *Resound: A Quarterly of the Archives of Traditional Music* 3, no. 4 (October): 5–6.

Christie, Agatha. 1926. *The Murder of Roger Ackroyd.* New York: Dodd, Mead, and Company.

Clarke, D. S. 1990. *Sources of Semiotic: Readings with Commentary from Antiquity to Present.* Carbondale: Southern Illinois University Press.

Clifford, James, and George E. Marcus. 1986. *Writing Culture: The Poetics and Politics of Ethnography*. Berkeley and Los Angeles: University of California Press.

Conot, Robert. 1979. *A Streak of Genius.* New York: Seaview Books.

Deacon, Desley. 1997. *Elsie Clews Parsons: Inventing Modernity.* Chicago: University of Chicago Press.

de Angelo, Jaime. 1973. *Indians in Overalls*. San Francisco: Turtle Island Press.

Deloria, Vine, Jr. 1969. *Custer Died for Your Sins: An Indian Manifesto*. New York: Macmillan.

Demetraeapoulou, D., and Cora DuBois. 1932. "A Study of Wintu Mythology." *Journal of American Folklore* 45:373–81.

Densmore, Frances. 1910. *Chippewa Music.* Bureau of American Ethnology Bulletin no. 45. Washington, D.C.: Smithsonian Institution.

———. [1917a] 1968. "Incidents in the Study of Ute Music." In *Frances Densmore and American Indian Music: A Memorial Volume,* ed. Charles Hofmann, 40, Contributions from the Museum of the American Indian, vol. 23. New York: Heye Foundation.

———. [1917b] 1968. "Study of Indian Music." In *Frances Densmore and American Indian Music: A Memorial Volume,* ed. Charles Hofmann, 101–14, Contributions from the Museum of the American Indian, vol. 23. New York: Heye Foundation.

———. 1940. Letter to Dr. John M. Cooper, 4 August 1940. Photocopy in the files of the Federal Cylinder Project, American Folklife Center, Library of Congress, Washington, D.C.

———. 1942. "The Study of Indian Music." In *Annual Report of the Board of Regents of the Smithsonian Institution for the Year 1941.* Washington, D.C.: Government Printing Office.

Deregowski, J. B. 1987. "Perception: Cultural Differences." In *The Oxford Companion to the Mind,* ed. Richard Langton Gregory, 601–2. Oxford: Oxford University Press.

Diamond, Stanley. 1964. "Nigerian Discovery: The Politics of Fieldwork." In *Reflections on Community Studies,* ed. Arthur J. Vidich, Joseph Bensman, and Maurice R. Stein. New York: John Wiley and Sons.

DuBois, Constance Goddard. 1908. "The Religion of the Luiseño Indians of Southern California." *University of California Publications in American Archaeology and Ethnology* 8:64–186.

Dundes, Alan. 1980. "Seeing Is Believing." In *Interpreting Folklore*, 86–92. Bloomington: Indiana University Press.

Edison, Thomas Alva. 1878. "The Phonograph and Its Future." *North American Review* 126 (June): 527–36.

Eisenstein, Elizabeth L. 1979. *The Printing Press as an Agent of Change.* Cambridge: Cambridge University Press.

Farrer, Claire. 1976. "Fieldwork Ethics." *Folklore Forum*, Bibliographic and Special Series 9:59–63.

Feld, Steven. 1982. *Sound and Sentiment: Birds, Weeping, Poetics, and Song in Kaluli Expression.* Philadelphia: University of Pennsylvania Press.

Fewkes, Jesse Walter. 1888. "The Perfected Phonograph." *North American Review* 146:641–50.

———. 1890a. "Additional Studies of Zuni Songs and Rituals with the Phonograph." *American Naturalist,* Nov., 1094–98.

———. 1890b. "A Contribution to Passamaquoddy Folklore." *Journal of American Folk-Lore* 3:257–80.

———. 1890c. "On the Use of the Phonograph in the Study of the Languages of American Indians." *Science* 2 (May): 267–69.

———. 1890d. "The Use of the Phonograph in the Study of the Languages of American Indians." *American Naturalist* 24:495–99.

———. 1890–1891. Fewkes Cylinder Collection, FCP 4,247. Federal Cylinder Project, American Folklife Center, Library of Congress, Washington, D.C.

———. 1891. "A Few Summer Ceremonials at Zuñi Pueblo. Hemenway Southwestern Archaeological Expedition." *Journal of American Ethnology and Archaeology* 1:1–61.

———. 1899. "Hopi Basket Dances." *Journal of American Folklore* 12:31–96.

Fillmore, John Comfort. 1895. "What Do Indians Mean to Do When They Sing, and How Far Do They Succeed?" *Journal of American Folk-Lore* 8:138–42.

Fine, Elizabeth C. 1984. *The Folklore Text: From Performance to Print.* Bloomington: Indiana University Press.

Fletcher, Alice Cunningham. 1893. "A Study of Omaha Indian Music." *Archaeological and Ethnological Papers of the Peabody Museum* 1, no. 5:231–82.

———. 1905. "The Hako: A Pawnee Ceremony." In *Bureau of American Ethnology Annual Report for the Year 1904*, pt. 2. Washington, D.C.: Government Printing Office.

Fontana, Bernard L. 1973. "Savage Anthropologists and the Unvanishing Indians of the American Southwest." *Indian Historian* 6 (Winter): 5–8.

Freilich, Morris. 1970. *Marginal Natives: Anthropologists at Work.* New York: Harper and Row.

Friedman, D. G. 1964. "Smiling in Blind Infants and the Issue of Innate Versus Acquired." *Journal of Child Psychology and Psychiatry* 5:171–84.

Gacs, Ute, et al. 1989. *Women Anthropologists: Selected Biographies.* Urbana and Chicago: University of Illinois Press.

Gallup, George H., Jr, and Frank Newport. 1991. "Belief in Paranormal Phenomena Among Adult Americans." *Skeptical Inquirer* 15 (Winter): 137–46.

Gelatt, Roland. 1977. *The Fabulous Phonograph,* rev. ed. New York: Macmillan.

Georges, Robert A., and Michael Owen Jones. 1980. *People Studying People: The Human Element in Fieldwork.* Berkeley and Los Angeles: University of California Press.

Gillis, Frank. 1984. "The Incunabula of Instantaneous Ethnomusicological Sound Recordings, 1890–1910: A Preliminary List." In *Problems and Solutions: Occasional Essays in Musicology Presented to Alice Moyle,* ed. J. Kassler and J. Stubington, 322–55. Sydney: Hale and Ironmonger.

Gilman, Benjamin Ives. 1891. "Zuni Melodies." *A Journal of American Ethnology and Archaeology* 1:63–91.

———. 1908. *Hopi Songs.* Boston: Houghton Mifflin.

Goldstein, Kenneth S. 1964. *A Guide for Fieldworkers in Folklore.* Hatboro, Pa.: Folklore Associates.

Grainger, Percy. 1909. "Collecting with the Phonograph." *Journal of the Folk-Song Society* 3:147–62.

Gray, Judith A. 1988. *Great Basin/Plateau Indian Catalog, Northwest Coast/Arctic Catalog.* Vol. 3:3 of *The Federal Cylinder Project: A Guide to Field Cylinder Collections in Federal Agencies,* Dorothy Sara Lee, gen. ed. Studies in American Folklife, no. 3:5. Washington, D.C.: American Folklife Center, Library of Congress.

Gray, Judith A., and Dorothy Sara Lee. 1985. *Northeastern Indian Catalog, Southeastern Indian Catalog.* Vol. 2 of *The Federal Cylinder Project: A Guide to Field Cylinder Collections in Federal*

Agencies, Dorothy Sara Lee, gen. ed. Studies in American Folklife, no. 3:2. Washington, D.C.: American Folklife Center, Library of Congress.

Gray, Judith A., and Edwin J. Schupman. 1984. *California Indian Catalog, Middle and South American Catalog, Southwestern Indian Catalog*—I. Vol. 5 of *The Federal Cylinder Project: A Guide to Field Cylinder Collections in Federal Agencies,* Dorothy Sara Lee, gen. ed. Studies in American Folklife, no. 3:5. Washington, D.C.: American Folklife Center, Library of Congress.

Grinnell, George Bird. 1907. "Some Early Cheyenne Tales." *Journal of American Folklore* 20:169–94.

Guillemin, Jeanne. 1975. *Urban Renegades: The Cultural Strategy of North American Indians.* New York: Columbia University Press.

Hall, Edward T. 1959. *The Silent Language.* Garden City, N.J.: Anchor Press.

Harris, Marvin. 1968. *The Rise of Anthropological Theory.* New York: Thomas Y. Crowell.

Hastings, Dennis. 1985. "Reflections on the Omaha Cylinder Recordings." Liner notes, *Omaha Indian Music: Historic Recordings from the Fletcher/La Flesche Collection,* Archive of Folk Culture Recording AFS 71. Washington, D.C.: American Folklife Center and Omaha Tribal Council.

Helmholtz, Hermann L. von. [1866] 1968. "Concerning the Perceptions in General." In *Helmholtz on Perception: Its Physiology and Development,* ed. and trans. Richard M. Warren and Roslyn P. Warren, 1171–203. New York: John Wiley and Sons.

———. [1881] 1968. "On the Relation of Optics to Painting." In *Helmholtz on Perception: Its Physiology and Development,* ed. and trans. Richard M. Warren and Roslyn P. Warren, 137–68. New York: John Wiley and Sons.

Herder, Johann Gottfried von. [1765] 1972. "Correspondence on Ossian and the Songs of Ancient People." In *The Rise of Modern Mythology,* 1680–1860, ed. and trans. Burton Feldman and Robert D. Richardson, 229–30. Bloomington: Indiana University Press.

Herskovits, Melville J. 1973. *Franz Boas.* Clifton, N.J.: Augustus M. Kelley.

Herskovits, Melville J., and Frances S. Herskovits. 1936. *Suriname Folk-Lore.* Columbia Contributions to Anthropology, no. 27. New York: Columbia University Press.

Herzog, George. 1936. "Research in Primitive and Folk Music in the United States." American Council of Learned Societies Bulletin no. 24. Washington, D.C..

Hinsley, Curtis M., Jr. 1976. "Amateurs and Professionals in Washington Anthropology, 1879 to 1903." In *American Anthropology: The Early Years,* ed. John V. Murra, pp. 36–68. St. Paul: West Publishing.

———. 1981. *Savages and Scientists: The Smithsonian Institution and the Development of American Anthropology, 1846–1910.* Washington, D.C.: Smithsonian Institution Press.

———. 1983. "Ethnographic Charisma and Scientific Routine: Cushing and Fewkes in the American Southwest, 1879–1893." In *Observers Observed: Essays on Ethnographic Fieldwork,* vol. 1 of History of Anthropology, ed. George Stocking Jr., 53–69. Madison: University of Wisconsin Press.

Hofmann, Charles, ed. 1968. *Frances Densmore and American Indian Music: A Memorial Volume,* Contributions from the Museum of the American Indian, vol. 23. New York: Heye Foundation.

Holmes, W. H. 1906. Letter, National Anthropological Archives. Photocopy in files of Federal Cylinder Project, American Folklife Center, Library of Congress, Washington, D.C.

Hymes, Dell. 1970. "Linguistic Method in Ethnography: Its Development in the United States." In *Method and Theory in Linguistics,* ed. P. L. Garvin, 249–311. The Hague: Mouton.

Institut Internationale de Coopération Intellectuelle. 1934. *Musiques et Chansons Populaires.* Paris: United Nations.

Jabbour, Alan. 1984. Preface to *Introduction and Inventory,* by Erika Brady et al. Vol. 1 of *The Federal Cylinder Project: A Guide to Field Cylinder Collections in Federal Agencies,* Dorothy Sara Lee, gen. ed. Studies in American Folklife, no. 3:1. Washington, D.C.: American Folklife Center, Library of Congress.

Jackson, Michael. 1989. *Paths Toward a Clearing: Radical Empiricism and Ethnographic Inquiry.* Bloomington and Indianapolis: Indiana University Press.

Jaynes, Julian. 1976. *The Origin of Consciousness in the Breakdown of the Bicameral Mind.* Boston: Houghton Mifflin.

Judd, Neil Merton. 1967. *The Bureau of American Ethnology: A Partial History.* Norman: University of Oklahoma Press.

Karpeles, Maude. 1967. *Cecil Sharp: His Life, His Work.* Chicago: University of Chicago Press.

Kodish, Debora. 1986. *Good Friends and Bad Enemies: Robert Winslow Gordon and the Study of American Folksong*. Urbana and Chicago: University of Illinois Press.

Krehbiel, H. E. 1891. Letter. *Musical Visitor* 20, no. 10 (1891): 256–57. Reprinted in Ethnomusicology 2 (1958): 116–17.

Kroeber, Theodora. 1970. *Alfred Kroeber: A Personal Configuration*. Berkeley and Los Angeles: University of California Press.

Kurin, Richard. 1997. *Reflections of a Culture Broker: A View from the Smithsonian*. Washington, D.C., and London: Smithsonian Institution Press.

La Flesche, Francis. 1927–1928. "Rite of the Wa-xo'-be and Shrine Degree." In *Bureau of American Ethnology Annual Report* 45:533–38.

———. 1915–18. Collection of Osage Indian Music, AFS. no. 20,200–20,209; 20218, 20,223–20,238. Archive of Folk Culture, American Folklife Center, Library of Congress.

Lansing, B. Bloom, ed. 1936. "Bourke on the Southwest." *New Mexico Historical Review* 11:203–4.

Lee, Dorothy Sara. 1984a. *Early Anthologies*. Vol. 8 of *The Federal Cylinder Project: A Guide to Field Cylinder Collections in Federal Agencies,* Dorothy Sara Lee, gen. ed. Studies in American Folklife, no. 3:8. Washington, D.C.: American Folklife Center, Library of Congress.

———. 1984b. "Field Report: Omaha Tribal Pow-wow, Macy, Nebraska, 10–13 August." Unpublished manuscript in the files of the Federal Cylinder Project, American Folklife Center, Library of Congress, Washington, D.C.

List, George. 1958a. "The Reproduction of Cylinder Recordings." *Folklore and Folk Music Archivist* 1, no. 2:7–8.

———. 1958b. "The Reproduction of Cylinder Recordings." *Folklore and Folk Music Archivist* 1, no. 3:11–12.

"Local Meetings and Other Notices." 1892. *Journal of American Folk-Lore* 5:158–59.

———. 1898. *Journal of American Folk-Lore* 11:79.

Lomax, Alan. 1971. *Folksong Style and Culture*. Washington, D.C.: American Association for the Advancement of Science.

Lomax, John Avery. 1937. "Field Experiences with Recording Machines." *Southern Folklore Quarterly* 1:58–59.

———. 1947. *Adventures of a Ballad Hunter*. New York: Macmillan.

Longford, Elizabeth. 1965. *Victoria: Born to Succeed*. New York: Harper and Row.

Lord, Albert B. 1960. *The Singer of Tales*. New York: Atheneum.

Lowie, Robert H. 1943. "Franz Boas, Anthropologist." *Scientific Monthly* 56:183–84.

———. [1956] 1972. "Reminiscences of Anthropological Currents in American Half a Century Ago." In *Robert H. Lowie,* ed. Robert F. Murphy, 78–108. New York: Columbia University Press. Reprinted from American Anthropologist 58 (1956): 995–1016.

———. 1959. *Robert H. Lowie, Ethnologist: A Personal Record.* Berkeley and Los Angeles: University of California Press.

Lurie, Nancy Oestreich. 1966a. "The Lady from Boston and the Omaha Indians." *American West* 3:31–33, 80–85.

———. 1966b. "Women in Early American Anthropology." In *Pioneers of American Anthropology: The Uses of Biography,* ed. June Helm, 54–64. Seattle: University of Washington Press.

Mach, Ernst. [1886] 1897. *Contributions to the Analysis of the Sensations,* trans. Cora May Williams. Chicago: Open Court. Reprinted as *The Analysis of Sensations,* trans. Cora May Williams. New York: Dover, 1959.

Mark, Joan. 1980. *Four Anthropologists: An American Science in Its Early Years.* New York: Science History Publications.

———. 1988. *Stranger in Her Native Land: Alice Fletcher and the American Indians.* Lincoln: University of Nebraska Press.

McLuhan, Marshall. 1962. *The Gutenberg Galaxy.* Toronto: University of Toronto Press.

Michelson, Truman. 1911–1917. Collection of Indian Music Recorded from Various Tribes, Piegan recordings. Archive of Folk Culture, AFS 20, 513–20, Washington, D.C., Library of Congress.

Morgan, Lewis Henry. 1877. *Ancient Society*. New York: Charles H. Kerr and Company.

Nash, Dennison. 1963. "The Ethnologist as Stranger: An Essay in the Sociology of Knowledge." *Southwestern Journal of Anthropology* 19:149–67.

Nash, Dennison, and Ronald Wintrob. 1972. "The Emergence of Self-Consciousness in Ethnography." *Current Anthropology* 13:527–42.

Needham, Rodney. [1967] 1979. "Percussion and Transition." In *Reader in Comparative Mythology,* 4th ed., ed. William Lessa and Evon Vogt, 311–37. New York: Harper Collins. Reprinted from *Man* 2:606–14.

Nequatewa, Edmund. 1980. "Dr. Fewkes and Masauwu." In *The Southwest Corner of Time: An Indian Literary Magazine,* ed.

Larry Evers, 36–37. Tucson, Ariz.: Suntracks.

O'Brien, Flann. 1974. *The Poor Mouth: A Bad Story About the Hard Life.* New York: Viking.

Ó Danachair, Caoimhín. 1951. *Laos* 1:180–86.

O'Meara, J. Tim. 1990. Review of *Paths to a Clearing: Radical Empiricism and Ethnographic Inquiry* by Michael Jackson. *Journal of Anthropological Research* 46:202–5.

Ong, Walter, S. J. 1967. *The Presence of the Word: Some Prolegmena for Cultural and Religious History.* New Haven: Yale University Press.

———. 1982. *Orality and Literacy.* New York: Methuen.

Ortiz, Alfonso. 1971. "An Indian Anthropologist's Perspective." *Indian Historian* 4:11–14.

Pandey, Trikoli Nath. 1972. "Anthropologists at Zuni." *Proceedings of the American Philosophical Society* 116, no. 4:321–37.

Paul, Benjamin D. 1953. "Interview Techniques and Field Relationships." In *Anthropology Today: An Encyclopedic Inventory,* ed. by Alfred Kroeber, 430–51. Chicago: University of Chicago Press.

Petts, Leonard. 1983. *The Story of Nipper and the His Master's Voice Picture,* 2nd rev. ed. Bournemouth, U.K.: Talking Machine Review.

The Phonograph and How to Use It. 1900. New York: National Phonograph Company.

Piaget, Jean, and Bärbel Inhelder. 1969. *The Psychology of the Child,* trans. Helen Weaver. New York: Basic Books.

Porterfield, Nolan. 1996. *Last Cavalier: The Life and Times of John A. Lomax.* Urbana and Chicago: University of Illinois Press.

Powell, John Wesley. 1880. "Sketch of Lewis H. Morgan." *Popular Science Monthly* 18:115.

Proudfoot, Christopher. 1980. *Collecting Phonographs and Gramophones.* New York: Mayflower.

Radin, Paul. 1949. *The Culture of the Winnebago: As Described by Themselves.* Special Publications of the Bollingen Foundation, no. 1. *International Journal of American Linguistics,* Memoir 2. Bloomington: Indiana University Publications in Anthropology and Linguistics.

Rainer, J. D., S. Abdullah, and J. C. Altshuler. 1970. "Phenomenology of Hallucinations in the Deaf." In *Origin and Mechanisms of Hallucinations,* ed. Wolfram Keup. New York: Plenum.

Read, Oliver, and Walter L. Welch. 1959. *From Tin Foil to Stereo.* Indianapolis: Bobbs-Merrill Company.

Reichard, Gladys. 1943. "Franz Boas and Folklore." In *Franz Boas, 1858–1942,* ed. Alfred L. Kroeber, 52–57. Memoirs of the American Anthropological Association 61. Menasha, Wisc.: American Anthropological Association.

Resek, Carl. 1960. *Lewis Henry Morgan, American Scholar.* Chicago: University of Chicago Press.

Revak, Nancy S. 1967. "The Evolution of Shorthand to 1967." Master's thesis, Kent State University.

Ritchie, Jean. 1963. *Singing Family of the Cumberlands.* New York: Oak Publications.

Roberts, Helen Heffron. 1925. "A Study of Folk Song Variants Based on Field Work in Jamaica." *Journal of American Folklore* 38:149–216.

———. 1926. Collection of Karok and Konimihu Indian Music, AFS no. 19,874–19,882, Archive of Folk Culture, American Folklife Center, Library of Congress.

———. 1931. "Suggestions to Field Workers in Collecting Folk Music and Data About Instruments." *Journal of the Polynesian Society* 40:111–12.

———. 1979. Interview conducted by Maria La Vigna and David P. McAllester, 5 December, Camden, Conn. Archive of Folk Culture AFS 19,894–19,899.

———. 1980. Selected cuts. *Na leo Hawai'i kahiko: Voices of Old Hawai'i.* Audio-recording Collections Series 1. Honolulu: Bernice P. Bishop Museum. Recorded from Helen Heffron Roberts Collection of Hawaiian Music, Archive of Folk Culture AFS Discs 759–73.

Roberts, Helen Heffron, and Robert Lachmann. [1935] 1963. "The Re-recording of Wax Cylinders." *Zeitschrift für vergleichende Musikwissenschaft* 3:75–83. Reprinted in *Folklore and Folk Music Archivist* 6:4–11.

Rowe, John Holland. 1953. "Technical Aids in Anthropology." In *An Appraisal of Anthropology Today,* ed. Alfred L. Kroeber, 914–17. Chicago: University of Chicago Press.

Ruby, Jay. 1982. *A Crack in the Mirror: Reflexive Perspectives in Anthropology.* Philadelphia: University of Pennsylvania Press.

Skinner, Alanson B. 1915. "The Value of Recording Indian Folklore." *Society of American Indians Quarterly Journal* 3:46–48.

Smith, Marion. 1959. "Boas' `Natural History' Approach to Field Method." In *The Anthropology of Franz Boas,* ed. Walter Goldschmidt, 46–60. American Anthropological Society Memoir no. 89. Menasha, Wisc.: American Anthropological Association.

Stewart, Edward C. 1972. *American Cultural Patterns: A Cross-Cultural Perspective.* Washington, D.C.: Society for Intercultural Education, Training, and Research.

Stocking, George W. 1974. "Introduction: The Basic Assumptions of Boasian Anthropology." In *The Shaping of American Anthropology: A Franz Boas Reader,* ed. George W. Stocking, 1–20. New York: Basic Books.

———, ed. 1983. *Observers Observed: Essays on Ethnographic Fieldwork.* Madison: University of Wisconsin Press.

———. 1992. *The Ethnographer's Magic, and Other Essays in the History of Anthropology.* Madison: University of Wisconsin Press.

Stoller, Paul. 1989. *The Taste of Ethnographic Things: The Senses in Anthropology.* Philadelphia: University of Pennsylvania Press.

Stone, Ruth. 1981. "Toward a Kpelle Conceptualization of Music Performance." *Journal of American Folklore* 94:188–206.

———. 1982. *Let the Inside Be Sweet: The Interpretation of Music Event Among the Kpelle of Liberia.* Bloomington: Indiana University Press.

Swanton, John R., and Helen Heffron Roberts. 1931. "Obituary: Jesse Walter Fewkes." *Annual Report of the Board of Regents of the Smithsonian Institution for the Year 1930.* Washington, D.C.: Government Printing Office.

Thompson, Stith. 1955–58. *Motif-Index of Folk-Literature,* rev. ed. Bloomington: Indiana University Press.

Toelken, Barre. 1976. "Seeing With a Native Eye: How Many Sheep Will It Hold?" In *Seeing With a Native Eye: Essays on Native American Religion,* ed. Walter Holden Capps, 9–24. New York: Harper Forum.

———. 1998. "The Yellowman Tapes, 1966–1997." *Journal of American Folklore* 111:381–91.

Twain, Mark. [1884–85] 1967. *Huckleberry Finn.* Indianapolis: Bobbs-Merrill.

Two Guns, Evelyn. 1915. "The Indian Fondness for Music." *Society of American Indians Quarterly Journal* 3:135–36.

Underhill, Ruth M. 1979. *Papago Woman.* New York: Holt Rinehart and Winston.

———. 1979. *Rain and Ocean: Speeches for the Papago Year.* American Tribal Religions, vol. 4. Tempe: Museum of Northern Arizona Press.

Van Maanen, John. 1988. *Tales of the Field: On Writing Ethnography.* Chicago: University of Chicago Press.

Vennum, Thomas Jr. 1984. "Who Should Have Access to Indian Music in Archives?" In *Sharing a Heritage: American Indian Arts,* 137–46. Los Angeles: American Indian Studies Center, University of California at Los Angeles.

Viola, Herman J. 1981. *Diplomats in Buckskins: A History of Indian Delegations in Washington City.* Washington, D.C.: Smithsonian Institution Press.

Warren, R. M., and R. P. Warren. 1968. *Helmholtz on Perception: Its Physiology and Development.* New York: John Wiley and Sons.

Wax, Rosalie H. 1971. *Doing Fieldwork: Warnings and Advice.* Chicago: University of Chicago Press.

Wertheimer, Michael. 1961. "Psychomotor Coordination of Auditory and Visual Space at Birth." *Science* 134:1692.

Wilgus, D. K. 1959. *Anglo-American Folksong Scholarship Since 1898.* New Brunswick: Rutgers University Press.

Wyman, Lorraine. 1920. "Songs from Perce." *Journal of American Folklore* 33:321–35.

Yates, Michael. 1982. "Percy Grainger and the Impact of the Phonograph." *Folk Music Journal* 4:265–75.

Zuckerkandl, Victor. 1956. *Sound and Symbol: Music and the External World,* New York: Pantheon.

Zumwalt, Rosemary Lévy. 1988. *American Folklore Scholarship: A Dialogue of Dissent.* Bloomington: Indiana University Press.

Index